A Workbook Series for Racial Justice Advocates

Stop Being Afraid!

5 Steps to Transform Your Conversations about Racism

Lean in & Plant a Seed

BOOK 1

BY DR. AMANDA KEMP

Series: Racial Justice from the H.E.A.R.T.   Volume 1

Racial Justice from the Heart Press

Lancaster, PA

Stop Being Afraid .

For information contact

Dr. Amanda Kemp LLC

342 N. Queen St.

Lancaster, PA 17603

The information contained in this book is for informational purposes only.

I am not a psychologist. You should always seek the advice of a professional before acting on something that I have published or recommended.

The material in this book may include information, products or services by third parties. Third Party Materials comprise of the products and opinions expressed by their owners. As such, I do not assume responsibility or liability for any Third Party material or opinions.

The publication of such Third Party Materials does not constitute my guarantee of any information, instruction, opinion, products or services contained within the Third Party Material. The use of recommended Third Party Material does not guarantee any success related to you. Publication of such Third Party Material is simply a recommendation and an expression of my own opinion of that material.

Praise for Dr. Amanda Kemp

Before working with Amanda I felt anxious and unclear about how to begin the work with and for my family. Now I feel encouraged, more clear and excited about next steps. In fact, I took a step by talking with my son about it this evening.

—*Joyce Inspira Williams, African American and Multicultural Counseling, New Jersey*

I'd been searching for years for writing and strategies for social justice that I could relate to on a spiritual level; you connected those things.

—*Natalie Sanchez, Breath of Fire Latina Theatre Ensemble*

I honestly don't believe I would have felt brave enough to show "Moonlight" before taking your class. I think this experience will transform my teaching and help me bring more empathy and understanding to the classroom, even as I push my students to discuss things that might make them uncomfortable.

—*Mick Teti-Beaudin, Professor, Harrisburg Area Community College*

The Scholars, to a person, found Amanda's writing and presence effective and challenging. I would also say that Amanda's approach and spirit opened for our group another way of discussing the asymmetrical nature of any/all dialogue on racism. Amanda's presence was a gift for us.

—*Mark Justad, Professor, Guilford College*

Thank you for the fantastic job you did guiding our racial justice course. I found the experience validating, unsettling and inspiring at once. The skills you taught us in the class—and also helped us to practice over and over—are skills I know I will be able to use in any important conversation, and especially those around race... It was also very empowering to see you model such great technique—seeing is believing.

—*Kim Warshawsky, Franklin & Marshall College*

One of the things I deeply appreciate about Amanda's approach is its foundation: Holding space for transformation – a meditative, prayerful practice of becoming part of the flow of unconditional love and unconditional acceptance. A challenging practice, to be sure, and it is also aligned with how I want to live and how I want to do this work.

—*Mary Kay Glazer, Quaker and North Carolina NAACP Executive Board Member*

A big aha moment for me was realizing that the bulk of my work is actually with WHITE people! Throughout my life I've been dedicating myself to being immersed in other cultures, learning about my own privilege and asking what to do, what to say and how to go about it. You helped me shift from asking people of color what I need to do, to realizing I need to have the courageous conversations with other people in power, people who look like me and thus are more likely to listen to me.

—*Summer Jasmine Lall, Music Therapist*

*This book is dedicated to people who stand
on the ground of justice and compassion.*

You were meant for this moment.

*Special thanks to Black women I've admired for their living examples of
openhearted wisdom and courage: the late great Aunt Bessie Brown,
Sonja Ahuja, and Jojopah Nsoroma.*

Table of Contents

PREFACE

This workbook grew out of three years of teaching Racial Justice from the Heart in person and online. It is based on a transcript from an extraordinary day-long retreat where we got real about our successes and failures to build a movement for change. We have included the actual dialogue from three European American participants, our European American senior trainer, and me, an African American teacher/healer/artist. The participant names have been changed to protect their privacy but the challenges, failures, and feelings are real.

I evolved Racial Justice from the Heart workshops and these Five Steps out of my lived experience as the mother of African American teens, as a partner in an interracial marriage to a European American man, and as a person committed to racial justice. These steps have helped me to say, "No," or, "Not now," to conversations when they were not in my best interest and to say, "Yes," to conversations when I was ready. They have helped me to practice a co-creation mindset and to love myself even when everything in the dominant culture would have me lash out or undermine my own values. These steps have stretched me and called me to be the change that I want to see.

Other folks have also benefited from these Five Steps. Teachers have used them in the classroom at the elementary and college levels, wives have used them to talk to husbands, Democrats to talk with Republican family members, and church members one to another. I've gotten unsolicited success emails from people as varied as Shayna, an African American educator who was getting burnt out from having the same conversations about racism with her European American colleagues, to Mick, a European American English professor who was afraid to facilitate a discussion about racism in her multiracial classroom because of past blowups.

Because the participants at the daylong retreat were European Americans who sought guidance on talking effectively with other European Americans, this workbook reflects that perspective. However, the steps can be used by people of color to talk with each other and to talk with people of European descent.

Because of the particular challenges and history of Black people in the U.S., I will soon publish another book in the series especially geared toward Black people. I am committed to the idea that Black people, especially Black change makers, adopt strategies for change that include taking care of our bodies and our hearts.

The series will also include two other books: *How to Hold Someone Accountable for Racism* and *How to Challenge an Expert in Public Forums*. My intention is that these books give folks conversational scaffolding so that they can stand and attract others to stand for racial justice. In the end, racial justice cannot be achieved without the participation of lots of people. What we know about change is that one conversation or interaction usually doesn't change a perspective. It takes repeated exposure, a feeling of respect, and a sense of inclusion in an alternative narrative which gives someone new ground to stand upon.

This workbook series is the natural extension of my first book *Say the Wrong Thing: Stories and Strategies for Racial Justice and Authentic Community*. Where Say the Wrong Thing emphasized stories and principles of racial justice, this workbook teaches you how you can immediately implement the Five Steps into your daily life and daily conversations. *Stop Being Afraid* can be used alone or in conjunction with our Racial Justice from the Heart courses. If there's one thing I can say for sure, it's that ALL of us need accountability and support. Difficult conversations take courage, clarity, and conscious emotional and physical self-care.

Thank you for being part of the movement to stand for justice and compassion.

Peace and love,
Amanda

INTRODUCTION

This book is divided into two parts: Part One introduces me and Erika Fitz and how we personally came to this work. It also provides an overview to the Five Steps to Transform your Conversations about Racism and reminds us of what does not work. We discuss a white frame of reference, white supremacy culture and distinguish between European ethnic identities and whiteness. Part Two contains one chapter on each of the Five Steps. Throughout the book you will find Action Steps and Worksheets. We encourage you to complete these so that the book can actually affect your behaviors.

You will see references to actions steps as you read. Please take the time to do them. I strongly recommend you get a journal and keep all of your responses, plans, and reflections on your conversations in one place. You will find that your answers will change over time as you get more deft at these conversations. Remember progress not perfection!

Finally, this work can be undertaken by groups. We recommend that you read small segments and leave plenty of time for discussion to get the most out of your efforts. I think that practice and reflection will teach you far more than theoretical conversations. So, if you decide to read this book in a group, see if you can each commit to practicing each step in your real life in between group sessions.

SECTION ONE

OVERVIEW OF THE FIVE STEPS AND THE RACIAL JUSTICE FROM THE HEART SYSTEM

Amanda:

So, welcome everybody to the virtual seminar on the Five Steps to Transform Your Conversations about Racism, especially the conversation where you are leaning in and planting seeds—so this all-day seminar is going to focus on that type of conversation. I want to start off by telling you that this virtual seminar is an opportunity for you to be in a community of committed folks.

About Dr. Amanda Kemp

So, I'll tell you a little bit about me in the context of doing Racial Justice from the HEART.

So I grew up in the Bronx, I'm in an interracial marriage right now. This is my second marriage. I have three European American teenagers and two African American teenagers, and what I'll say is that if anybody's ever brought together families within those age groups and across race lines and culture, class, it's been a journey. And what I noticed was that I had greater capacity to be patient and to be connected and to distinguish what was mine—what was mine to own and work with and what was someone else's—when I started to go to this self compassion class. So this is like four years ago.

Spirituality, Self-Compassion, and Justice

So I've been involved in racial justice work for most of my adult life, I guess all of my adult life, actually, so it's been like 30 plus years, but self compassion was new to me. Spirituality wasn't new to me, but self compassion was new to me. And as I started practicing more self compassion, I had more spaciousness to be with the conflicts and the differences that were emerging in my home that were simultaneously emerging in America.

The Political is Personal

This is around the time that Mike Brown was killed and Ferguson exploded or, you know, maybe explode is the wrong word but Ferguson got in action and in motion to demand justice, and all of that—the killing of Eric Garner, and the people not being you know, held accountable—all that sort of increased my anxiousness for my children who are Black, and my anger and my sorrow—all of that was rising at the same time. And I found that these self compassion techniques that I was learning—what I was learning about the brain, and wholeheartedness, and mindfulness—came at the right time. It just helped me to see how I was contributing to my suffering. So, if you're on this call you know that we live in an unjust and oppressive society, you know that we live in a toxic, white supremacist, misogynistic, homophobic, patriarchal, piece of BS.

And we're here. We are here. You know, I'm not leaving yet. And I have people who I'm responsible for, who I care deeply about. So that's another reason why I'm not leaving yet, right? Well, then how do I be here, how do I be an effective change maker given this context? So what emerged for me was holding, standing for justice, *cultivating* justice and compassion, *cultivating* compassion within me, bringing forward *both* of those simultaneously inextricably, keeping them linked. So, that opening up led to *Say the Wrong Thing*, the book that I published where I first laid out Racial Justice from the HEART as a system. So I wrote this book, which was my experience—short essays on my lived experience within my interracial household, dealing with all the pain of this moment. And I saw some strategies. I knew it had to do with the heart, so I saw some things that I was doing, that were helpful, that I wanted to share with other people.

Introducing Dr. Erika Fitz, Senior Trainer

Amanda:

So I just started to share, I just started to teach about that and that's where Erika came in. In my community where I live in Lancaster, I offered this series of five workshops on Racial Justice from the HEART, and I was asking Erika if she knew anybody who could support me, and she said, "*I could do it.*" And I was like, "You have a PhD in the Hebrew Bible—I mean don't you have to be doing that somewhere?" And luckily, she had just quit something that really wasn't aligned with her, and so she had some space. So we've been working together for three years, and Erika is now going to support us on this call in this capacity, and she's also a senior trainer in Racial Justice from the HEART.

Why Did You Sign Up for This Course?

Amanda:

So, I want to take a breath there because I think I've shared a lot actually, so now I'm going to ask you to share what made you come here this morning. What had you come? And I'm just going to put you in a random pair, you'll be with somebody else and you have like, you know, a minute and a half roughly, just to share what was there. So it doesn't have to be long, it doesn't have to be deep, but it could be deep. It just won't be long. Okay.

ACTION STEP:

Take a minute to write in your journal: Why did you decide to do this course? You can talk about why you wanted to do this specific course, or why you are motivated to work at racial justice more broadly.

Racial Justice from the HEART—the System

Amanda:

So this seminar is focusing on how to have a difficult or how to transform your conversation about racism specifically by leaning in and planting a seed. But this is part of a larger system for how to create more racial justice and diversity in your life, so I want to share with you just a quick peek at the overall system. So in Racial Justice from the HEART, the H is for Holding Space for Transformation. This the foundation of what we do. *And* it's for Having Difficult Conversations about Racism—for having conversations with people who don't already agree with you. To do that takes some skill.

Okay. So, Hold Space for Transformation is our foundation and it's also critical that we use it for Having Difficult Conversations about Racism with people we don't already agree with. And we're going to be focusing on that today.

We are also, if you scroll down you'll see the R, Reflect on Yourself, we are going to be using that strategy today, when we get to Step Four and Five in our five-part conversation that we are learning about. It's going to require some reflecting on ourselves, our internalized racism, our internalized implicit racial bias—reflecting on our experiences, our feelings.

So I wanted you to see overall that what we're doing today fits into part of a larger system for change.

Why Be Compassionate with a Racist?

Amanda:

So let's start off by talking about these difficult conversations about racism that we have. What I noticed was that after I had been practicing self-compassion work, that I was more willing to engage in conversations with people who I knew disagreed with me. For example, I had a co-worker who said he wanted to talk with me about Black Lives Matter. He was a European American man, that I wasn't friends with, but who knew what I do. And once I had enough accumulated goodness, soothing, healing, I was able to have that conversation with him. And I noticed that it went differently than other conversations I've had with people. One, because I didn't try to argue with him. I didn't try to convince his mind or his intellect that he was wrong and that I was right. Number two, I didn't exhaust myself. I didn't put a whole bunch of emotional energy out there, I didn't ask him to listen to me.

I didn't presume he was going to listen to me, I asked him before I shared my experience. And I found that by not going to refute his arguments, I found by being in this very yummy, heart-centered place, and by not offering my wisdom until he wanted it, that I had a whole different experience of the conversation. And I started thinking about how when you shift your listening and your intention, then what you get is something different.

What *Doesn't* Work: Why Most Conversations Fail

Self-righteousness

Amanda:

So, I want to turn our attention to the chat. Love all the stuff that came up here. And I wanted to comment on a few

of the things. So, Debbie wrote, "What hasn't worked is when I allow anger and self-righteousness to take

over, I find myself squishing white people who might otherwise be able to move more.", . I just want to

say, "!" Because when self-righteousness and anger take over, there's almost no feeling for the other

person. Have you noticed that? It's like—oof! You're just enveloped, right? And it's disconnecting. And it

can be kinda like a drug, you know? You can get addicted to self-righteousness—and anger, too—as a way

of protecting yourself. Can you say more about that, Debbie?

Debbie:

I was thinking about it and finding myself wanting to add it to the list of things that white people do in the white

fragility list. 'Cause that's what I do. I'm not guilty of white women's tears, but (of) that self righteous

anger—and it's actually getting in the way of the work.

Amanda:

Mm-hmm (affirmative). And this thing about *squishing* white people. There is a bit of *power over* isn't it? "I'm

going to dominate you," with my, my energy. Mm-hmm (affirmative).

11

Erika:

My "knowing-better-than-you."

Amanda:

Mm-hmm (affirmative). Put your hand up if you've been there, if you've done the self-righteous, squishing-other-people thing. I mean, I just did it last week to my neighbor honestly, so...thanks. So I'm glad you're here. That's awesome. Someone came to one of my workshops. She's a minister, worked with youth, and she came precisely for this: she was squishing people in her UU congregation. So she was preventing nasty things from being said, but she wasn't moving people. It was just creating more silence.

Pointing Out What the Other Person Did Wrong

Amanda:

Then Daniel says, "Starting with the description of what I think he did wrong just triggered defensiveness." Yep. You want to say any more about that, Daniel?

Daniel:

I was actually in a class a while ago, where the teacher advised us to "butter up" the person before we corrected them.

Amanda:

Thank you. I want to get to that thing about being honest and not being honest: "buttering up" or being straightforward. So this conversation that we're learning today is the "Lean In and Plant a Seed" type. But there is also what I would call an "accountability conversation." And with that conversation, describing what the person did that you think was wrong or harmful or racist or whatever, that is important. It doesn't come first, true. But it does come. It does come out.

And I just want to say: just because someone feels defensive doesn't mean that the game is over, or that you can't go back. Sometimes it can be useful to let someone sit with their defensiveness. But—or *and*—we don't want our defensiveness running the show.

Daniel:

Okay.

Amanda:

And sometimes when we call something racist or sexist or whatever, and someone has a defensive reaction, then what rises up is defensiveness inside of us. And then we got two walls. In the accountability conversation we practice how to not get *yourself* triggered into defensiveness. So then you've got another wall. We won't practice accountability conversations today, but you will get a chance to uncover your triggers.

We'll come back to buttering people up when we'll get to Step Three. Did you want to add something, Erika?

Erika:

I was in a role play in which someone used the term 'quota' about affirmative action, and I said, in what I thought was a gentle way, 'Well, it's my understanding that we don't actually use quotas, but I'd like to understand how you see it.' And it went very badly.

By starting with the specific, "Well, I differ with you on this particular thing," it just sent us off on this trajectory that after that point she was like, "Well, I'm going to fight you now." And it just kept us from getting down deeper to the heart level. I think political liberals really love their facts, and it was so hard for me to let go of the, "I need to set you straight on this." And I just should have. It wasn't the place to start at all.

I needed to find the thing that was in the heart level to connect to and let those other things go, for the moment at least. For that kind of conversation. Because it wasn't one where the stakes were high. It was one where I could have listened, but there was something in me that had to correct the facts, and I thought I was doing it really non defensively, but that wasn't the feedback. So I think you have to let the facts go for a minute sometimes and listen deeper.

Amanda:

Thank you. Thanks, Erika. Because we do know that. All we have to do is look at politics and elections to know that facts don't carry the day. They just don't carry the day. They are important. I think the truth is important—*and* it doesn't carry the day. What's the deeper truth? And that's below the level of facts. And I just want to say something about our role plays, since we are going to do some role playing today. It's a role play *and* it's real. For your subconscious, it's real. For your nervous system, it's real. So practicing in a role play is building up your racial stamina. It is building up your racial stamina by doing these role plays and being very conscious about what you're doing, and getting feedback from other people who are outside of you. So we're going to do that today. Thank you.

Thanks, Erika. That's a really good example.

Sam:

I learned that "gotcha/callout" method definitely doesn't produce good outcomes. So this was actually a conversation on Facebook. Conversations on Facebook, you're never going to change anybody's mind on Facebook anyway, but I posted a review of Michelle Obama's book by a Black woman who was, rather than being the, "Oh my God, this is the best book ever"—which it is a really good book—she, in addition to that, she said, "This is a great book *and* I really wish that Michelle Obama would bring some of her energy into really exploring and lifting up the difficulties that many Black women are struggling with that she isn't because she's Michelle Obama."

And then a lot of white people started jumping all over it—that anyone would ever say anything not-completely-adulatory about Michelle Obama. And this one friend of mine, who's white, posted a statement that she said, "If more Black people would approach race issues the way Michelle Obama does, we wouldn't have a problem in this country." (Laughs.) Actually, both another friend of mine and I just went, "Wow. That that is a wow statement that you just can't leave up there without some sort of response." I said something like, "Wow. That statement—do you see how that is a racist statement?" I said, 'That's a racist statement.' The person got super defensive and said, 'I am not a racist.' Which is not what I said, but it is what they heard.

And she went off on it. And then this other friend of mine chimed in trying to explain to her what's the difference between a racist statement and calling someone a racist, and why this statement was racist—naming all Black people in saying, "if only everyone was like Michelle Obama, we wouldn't have race problems in this country." It was so out there. And this is a very gentle, lovely, white, Buddhist-Quaker person, who of course is not racist...

Amanda:

Can I comment?

Sam:

Yes.

Amanda:

Okay. This is more like what I might call a Challenge type of conversation.

Sam:

Yeah.

Amanda:

So first of all, I think, like I said, some things you shut down.

Sam:

Yeah.

Amanda:

Right? So this was not a one-on-one conversation you were having with her. This was a public broadcast on your

platform.

Sam:

Yeah.

Amanda:

So for you to not have spoken about it very clearly and definitively then maybe implied something about you.

Sam:

Yes. Yes.

Amanda:

Or about...

Sam:

That I think that she's right. Yeah.

Amanda:

Right.

Sam:

That it's acceptable to say that.

Amanda:

Right. So that's one thing. And the second thing is that Facebook is not a place to practice Leaning In. It's a place to

broadcast. It's the place to have clashes. It's the place to say, "I hear you, high five." But it's not a place to

Lean In.

Sam:

Right, right.

Amanda:

It's the place where you could say, "Would you like to take this offline? 'Cause I'd like to talk with you about it."
And someone actually texted me in our Racial Justice from the Heart community, saying, "Hey, I ask someone to talk offline, and now I'm going to speak with this guy in a couple of hours. Wish me luck." Or something like that. So I was like, "Good!"

Sam:

Yeah.

Amanda:

So what I want to clarify is that it's okay to shut things down when it's your responsibility in some way.

Sam:

Yeah.

Amanda:

AND if you want to Lean In, then you can't do it online or via email because those aren't real-time, heart-to-heart communications. You get what I'm saying, right?

Sam:

Yeah.

Amanda:

Yeah.

Sam:

Yeah.

Amanda:

Wow. And that's so deep. The whole Michelle Obama thing, I mean, wow. She stirs up...I mean, people get used, *weaponized*. Have you heard about weaponizing people of color?

Sam:

Yeah.

Amanda:

Against each other. Somebody tried to use me in a conflict, a local conflict. Yeah. That's all I have to say about that.

Oh, and I do want to say something else, Sam, about, "I didn't say you were racist. That was a racist statement." I feel like there's something dishonest about it. Because I know you, so I know how you understand racism. And so you *do* think she's racist.

Sam:

Right. I think *I'm* racist. I know I'm racist.

Amanda:

Exactly. Exactly.

Sam:

That would be a long term conversation.

Amanda:

Right. That wouldn't be in an email or a Facebook comment. But if you're talking to someone and they're like, "Well, why are you calling me a racist?" Saying, "I didn't call you a racist. I said the statement was racist." Is not going to the heart of it. It's a little bit of a defensive move. "You're racist." "I didn't say..." "Your *statement's* racist. I didn't say *you* were racist." It's almost like a cover-your-ass move. And sometimes it's an important distinction to make, but I actually think that since you really do think that, and your understanding of racism is that everyone is a racist in some sense, then people *feel* it.

Sam:

Yes, you're right.

Amanda:

I wonder what other folks are hearing? So Sam, let's give some other people a chance to say what's rising up for them and then if you want, you can add anything.

Debbie:

I've been struggling with this term of "what's a racist statement?" and "who's racist?" It's like that little phrase has gotten confusing and it's triggering defensiveness. And I've been experimenting saying something like, "That statement really makes a generalization," or, "That statement really puts the blame on Black people. Can you hear where you're doing that?" It's actually avoiding the use of the word *racist* because you can come back to it later and say, "My assumption is that we're all operating in a racist society. That's not really what this conversation's about. My conversation is about the consequences of what you just said right them." I've been experimenting with that a bit.

Amanda:

Awesome. Thank you for sharing that. And how did it go when you made that switch?

Debbie:

When I am calm, I have been way more successful. When I'm feeling hot under the collar, I'm not doing well, but when I'm speaking with people who I already have a good relationship of trust with, I think that that's working quite well. Sometimes I get it right, but that little trick of, "let's not talk right now about who or what is racist, let's talk about what's going on really." I think that's really helpful.

Amanda:

Awesome. Thank you. Erika?

Erika:

I think what you're putting your finger on is that labeling something "racist" is like claiming a power in a cultural conversation that somebody knows is a weapon that can be used against them.

So, the label "racist" is a label that's like cultural dynamite and it can be weaponized in different ways. And if you're able to describe the behavior sort of more specifically, you can sidestep some of that. And I think Debbie, the way you said that was so helpful. Because it points out exactly *why* it's problematic, rather than giving it a label that somebody will be afraid is being used against them, and boxing them into a certain identity that *of course* they don't want to have. So I think that's really helpful, to reframe it that way.

Amanda:

Great. Thank you. Sam, did you want to add anything to that? Or are you good?

Sam:

No, I just think those responses were really helpful and thanks a lot.

Amanda:

And I just want to say—calling something racist is like a shorthand. And then people have different definitions of racist or racism. So I even say things like "white centered," "white supremacist," which a lot of people are like, "What the hell is that?" Which is okay. Thank you, Debbie. I mean, you do what works, right? And I have found that sometimes it's more precise to say, "That is white-centered," or, "That is Eurocentric."

Listening vs. Convincing

So today, what we're going to do is go through the Five Steps in a conversation that have worked for me. And if you have stuff that's worked for you, I always say, keep doing what works for you. You know what's organic to you, and what works, keep doing it. But if you're on this call, I'm assuming that you want a little more or maybe you want a lot more because something's not working right.

So today, I'm not going to tell you how to refute somebody's script, but instead, I'm going to show you how you can defuse it, how you can get them going deeper than the script without exhausting yourself, by using primarily your listening, and secondarily your own words.

So we think it's about, "Oh, I got to find the right thing to say," "I've got to say the right thing." And actually, more emphasis on your *listening*, secondarily on what you say, is what will have a bigger impact.

ACTION STEP:

Complete the worksheet **"Finding What Works"** below.

WORKSHEET: Finding What Works

Many people are skeptical of the idea of listening out a person with racist ideas. "Aren't I sending the message that I agree with them? That what they're saying is ok?" We feel like we're betraying our values. Or that we simply need to set the person straight on what they've got factually wrong.

Ok. So let's say that the person does have some things wrong. What will be the most effective way of having them change their mind?

Exercise:

1. Think about a time that you have made some shift in your own thinking after a conversation with someone. What allowed or helped that to happen?

_____

_____

_____

_____

2. Think about a conversation where you tried to shift someone else's thinking and it clearly did not work. What happened? Why didn't it work?

_____

_____

_____

_____

3. In your experience, what are some of the factors that make it more likely for a person to have a shift of attitude? What factors make it less likely?

_____

_____

_____

The White Script and White Frame of Reference

ACTION STEP:

Watch the video "Deconstructing White Privilege" and complete the worksheet below.

Worksheet: Deconstructing White Privilege

Watch this video, "Deconstructing White Privilege" by Dr. Robin DiAngelo: https://vimeo.com/147760743 and answer the following questions.

1. What does DiAngelo name as the "pillars" that support the narrative of a superficial equality ("race doesn't matter"/ "we're all the same")? (9:04)

_____

_____

_____

_____

_____

2. What examples have you seen or heard of "the white script"—ways that European Americans minimize or deny that racism is a current reality?

_____

_____

_____

_____

3. How does segregation perpetuate racial inequality in our culture? Why?

_____

_____

_____

_____

4. What does DiAngelo identify as the consequence of the "good/bad binary"? (from 16:45)?

_____

_____

_____

_____

5. Where do you encounter people of color in your everyday life?

_____

_____

_____

_____

6. Where do you encounter European Americans?

_____

_____

_____

_____

7. With how many of each do you have close, sustained relationships?

_____

_____

_____

8. What is the racial composition of your neighborhood? (Use percentages.)

_____

...of your workplace? _____

...of your local school or children's school? _____

...of your faith community or other social circles?

_____

9. After listening to DiAngelo's talk, what is one thing you might do, say, or notice differently?

_____

_____

_____

_____

_____

The White Script and White Frame of Reference (continued)

Amanda:

So I asked you to check out that Robin DiAngelo video [1] ("Deconstructing White Privilege") and inside of it she talks about a "white script." And by that, she's referring to the predictable things that people of European descent in the United States will say when confronted with a conversation about racism, or with an event that has racial undertones overtones to it.

Some things that she points out would be like, "I don't care if you're red, black, or brown, or pink, or purple." She said something like, "I can't be racist because my dad was racist, and I'm so not like him," or, "I can't be racist because my parents were in the Civil Rights movement, so I'm not racist,"—I'm sure you get the flavor, right? You're familiar with this white script.

What is a "White Script"?

Amanda:

So many of us get hooked into the white script and then we try to change somebody's mind. But they have been conditioned by that script over a long period of time. Sometimes we have a belief that in this ten-minute, five-minute, twenty-minute conversation, I'm going to shake you loose from those moorings—from those things that have given you stability (if you're European American)—about how America works, or how racism works." So I wanted us to look at what she said and focus on the white script when you're viewing her video because number one, I wanted us to be aware: it's a *script*—it's something that's very easy for people to fall into. It's just part of their conditioning. So it's not necessarily even like something they've thought deeply about, per se.

And number two, I also want us to become aware of where we get triggered in the script. You know—which of those things that get said, kind of catch us right *here* (motions to chest), you know? Or even lower. And you know, on the inside, we just can't even respond anymore; we're having a big internal reaction. I want us to be aware of that because when you know what your triggers are, then you can actually take some action to desensitize or neutralize those triggers. But if you don't know where they are, and you're not even thinking about them as triggers, and you're just constantly you know, having an internal or maybe an external reaction that derails you in the conversation.

White Frame of Reference

Amanda:

[DiAngelo also] talked about having a white frame of reference. And some people have a hard time defining what that is. And I'm sure what I'm going to say now isn't necessarily what she would say. But I want to clue you in on something that was very helpful to me.

Individual vs. group lenses

Amanda:

The way we've been socialized to think about race in this country and about ourselves is very different. European American folks tend to think of themselves as individuals, right? They experience life as an individual; they're being judged on their individual merit or lack of merit. This may not be not the case for White people who have other intersectional identities where they get marginalized, but on race, European Americans, they generally tend to think of themselves as individuals. People of color on the other hand, especially African Americans, because of our history in this country, and how legislation and all kinds of other stuff was created, we tend to think of ourselves very strongly as being part of a *group*—as having a group identity. We tend to think more about historical or societal trends.

So when you bring somebody who's thinking about racism on an individual level, into a conversation with somebody who's thinking about it on a societal, historical, or group level, they can both be having something truthful to say but be completely missing each other. So, let's see if I can come up with an example for you? Someone white might say "I think there are a lot of good police out there, Amanda. You know the police have been very helpful for me," or, "I never had any problems," or, "I think they work really hard," right? So it's coming from an individual level, and they are willing to give the police the benefit of the doubt, because of their individual level experience. There's really not been much negative there.

On the other hand, if you have a group identity as an African American, it doesn't matter if you've had individual experience with law enforcement, you're perceiving them, and you're being perceived *by them,* as a member of a group. And because you're part of this group—this racial group that is widely pictured as dangerous, criminal, shady, less than—then you will probably feel more vulnerable in your interaction with law enforcement, and they're going to feel more vulnerable with you, because of the ways that we've been implicitly trained to view Blackness.

So if you have someone who's talking about something from an individual level, and you have someone else who's talking about a group experience, and the person who's speaking on an individual level won't see a historical or group thing, then you're just going to have a constant conflict because they're coming from two different places.

Questions and Reflections:

Amanda:

So let me pause there because I would love to hear what's rising for you, especially on that point about a white frame of reference. But if you'd also like to comment on the script, I'd be open to that too. Anybody who has anything to say? And if you just raise your physical hand then I'll call you, and you can unmute yourself. Awesome. Erika, go ahead and unmute yourself.

Erika:

In the example that you gave of individual versus group perspectives, I can easily imagine being triggered by the fact that the other person, the white person, has the *luxury* to view it that way, you know? That they don't *have* to see what it's like from the other side—to be labeled and be part of a group, you know, so in addition to the injustice itself, there's the negation of your reality.

Amanda:

Right. Which is then why you get people saying things like, "Why are you so angry?" Or like, "I'm feeling a lot of energy!" My husband, who's European American, he'll be like, "Baby why are you yelling at me?" And I'm like, "I'm not yelling, I am *intense!"* And I think the fact that it's a different point of view, *and*—like what you said Erika—that *negating* of that very painful experience, it kind of compounds it. Which is why it's so great that the folks who are on this call are of European American descent, because there is a distance that you have from your lived experience that makes you more *able* to engage in this conversation without the same kind of emotional and psychological wearing, you know, tearing down.

Amanda:

Debbie.

Debbie:

What you said about European culture identified individually and people of color, particularly Black people, having a group mentality really resonates for me. I was reflecting on a conversation I had with an individual white police officer about race last year, and found myself trying to use the word "systematic oppression" with her in order to point out to her that nothing that I was saying was about her behavior, but that there was a systemic issue, and it was somewhat helpful.

I have a question for you. You said, "White people tend to think about it as an individual and people of color, particularly African Americans, as a group." Do you see that as something which is about historical culture, or is that a matter just of privilege?

Amanda:

Do I see it as a matter of culture or privilege, is that what you said?

Debbie:

That is what I said, I'm not sure whether that's clear.

Amanda:

Tell me what you mean, when you distinguish between those two things, just so I know.

Debbie:

Well, I think it's possible to make cultural distinctions like, observation of Asian cultures suggest that people who grew up there tend to think collectively—for example—and that might be said to be cultural rather than as a result of systematic oppression. So my question is: Is the fact that white people tend to think as individuals, is that about the history of individualistic European culture, or is it really only about the fact that they get the luxury to do so?

Amanda:

I think that's a good question. Oh, Sam wants to answer. Okay. Go ahead, Sam.

Sam:

I don't know if I have an answer, but I have ideas about that. I think it's really interesting. I think in this culture, the sort of American story, the myth that I grew up with was that I could pull myself up by my own bootstraps, that you know, Horatio Alger, you-can-do-it, and everything-I-achieved-is-mine. And so if that's a "white frame of reference," then any suggestion that there might be something that I have that I didn't personally earn is really threatening to my sense of identity and self-worth. But I think, and you know, I'm sort of presuming but from what I've read and learned, African Americans have definitely been oppressed, fighting for literally life and survival, and have done that through community. Community has been an important way of support and survival, but also, there's so much defined by the group experience that puts Amanda as an individual in *danger* when she just walks down the street.

So, I think that it's sort of a combination of both African American culture is more community-oriented *and* that whiteness has forced African Americans to see themselves as a group—this system of white supremacy system—that has created this culture.

Whiteness vs. European Ethnic Identities

Amanda:

I love this discussion because in some ways it's asking us to distinguish between whiteness, white supremacy and, you know, European cultures of which there are many, and European American cultures, of which there are also many. Debbie, I think where I would leave it is that we distinguish between whiteness and individual European heritages. You know what I mean? (This is something we discuss in our online class, Racial Justice from the Heart for European Americans.) Because whiteness was only created to dominate. It was really created to dominate and to justify domination but not just of people who are of African descent, and other people of color, but of other European people who then in the U.S. got seduced into, punished into, fled into, banged on the door to be let into whiteness—because it's so awful when you're not in that.

But it is a system of domination and it's Anglo-dominate with certain values. And Sam, individualism is definitely one of them. So let's leave it right there, but if you want to have more on that, contact us about the course.

Using the Five Steps: An Example from Real, Messy Life

Amanda:

I want to make myself vulnerable and share something with you. So, I recently had an interaction with a neighbor, a European American neighbor, a man, where he made a request, and I kind of blew up. Like, literally I felt like there was just flames coming from the top of my head, you know? I couldn't ... I didn't remember any of these steps I was just like, "Wow." It was like all the energy was right here. I was like a train, you know? I was just going full out. I was talking to Erika maybe a day later, and I shared just how embarrassed I felt. Not because I felt like what he said was right, but I felt embarrassed that, "Wow, I'm out of integrity with myself. I didn't even listen to him really." You know? I just had my big ol' reaction.

And it was really good to share it with Erika because it took it out of my head and into another human being. And when I took it to Erika, she knows what I'm standing for. So, I know she's not going to judge me, but I also know she's not going to go, "Yeah, well you should've told him this, too." She knows what I'm interested in is being grounded, being compassionate to myself and to other people, being truthful. When I shared my failure with her, because her listening was so beautiful, I started to laugh at myself. You know, I could hold it more lightly. And I said, "You know, okay, by next week, I'm going to have a talk with this neighbor again and I'm going to have apologized." So, that felt good, you know?

Then I was teaching a class that night, so I told the class, you know? *I told on myself,* and I think it's a very good thing to tell on yourself to people who know what you're about.

And, days start to go by and the pressure creeps up, because I still haven't gone over to talk to the neighbor. I asked my husband Michael to go with me. And he doesn't want to but he's willing to, because I gave him the look like, *This is when you need to step up.* So he's like, "Okay."

And then, over those days, I put all this pressure on myself. I started shaming myself some more. "I'm a fraud. I'm a bad person." "No, no, no, I'm not bad; *he's* bad. He should have never have said blah blah blah."

So I went back and forth between basically, "I'm wrong," "He's wrong," "I'm wrong," "He's wrong," for a couple of days. And what I noticed was that I actually felt bad both ways, even when I said he was wrong in my mind. I still felt kinda sick to my stomach. Putting the wrongness on it wasn't really getting me anywhere and it was making me feel bad. It was like extending my suffering.

Thankfully, that week I was in a self-compassion class, and I was just reminded to connect with something bigger than my fear. Because every time I thought about going over there and having a conversation with him, I got afraid. "Will they call the police on me?" "Will they slam the door in my face?" "Will they tell me off?" You know, I just didn't want to have bad things happen to me. So, when I got in touch with, "Okay, those are my fears *and* there's something bigger than my fear. There's something way, way bigger than my fear. And that something is with me that loves me."

All of a sudden I saw how beautiful and big the blue sky was. And that day, which was the deadline I had given myself, I knew I was going to go over and talk to the neighbor.

One other piece I wanted to share with you. I also needed to honor how hurt I had been by what the neighbor had said. Even if he didn't mean it or whatever, even if I misinterpreted it, I had felt pain. So I couldn't go back to the neighbor without also being with my pain. You know? Like really befriending myself as someone who was also in pain.

And then, I saw the blue sky, I realized I had my bigger connection. My husband Michael walked through the door and I was like, "Oh, you're just in time. I want to go talk to the neighbor." And he was like, "Well, what do I have to do?" I said, "Hold Space for Transformation." He's like, "Okay."

So, we went over there and the man who had spoken to me wasn't there, but his wife answered and she said, "He's at work." And I said, "Oh okay, well I'm Amanda, I'm your neighbor. And I really came over because I wanted to apologize. Your husband said something to me and I really didn't listen. I just had a big reaction, and I just blew up, and I'm sorry. And I just want you guys to know I—we—really want to be good neighbors. And I realize we don't even know you guys." You know, anyway, you get the flow of how it went. And then this lady started talking to me, and saying how she was working 12-hour shifts, and she has a baby under two, and she really wants to be home, and she said, "You know, I spoke to your husband like six months ago, and I'm really sorry 'cause I think I just was completely...I don't know what her word was, but out-of-line with him. And Michael said, "Yeah."

And we just kinda had this exchange of sharing more and more about what we were going through, you know? And why it had been hard for us. And then at the very end, Michael said, "Well, I'm sorry, too." I was looking at him like, "Why is he apologizing?" But he just felt like adding to it, you know? Because it was a very heartfelt moment. It was like letting go of who's wrong and who's right and instead, "What do I really want?"

I got clear: I want to be a good neighbor, you know, and I'm responsible. I'm able to be a good neighbor, but I wasn't in the previous interaction.

So, I tell you that long story because I want you to know that this is a practice, what I'm sharing with you, it's a practice. And even if you screw up the first time, you can return to it. You don't have to get it perfect. And it's a practice that's going to affect your own growth and expansion and transformation. Maybe even more

SECTION TWO

STEP ONE: CHECK IN WITH YOUR WISE SELF

Amanda:

Taking a breath. Okay. So, I'm going to take us to the first step in having a conversation with someone that you know you disagree with about racism. I'm going to take you to that first step, and that first step is to, before you begin, to check in with your wise self. Check in with your wise self.

If you are hurting, if you are anxious, if you are physically in pain, or you have to use the bathroom, or you're super hungry, or you're exhausted, I actually recommend you disengage and go take care of yourself.

Having a difficult conversation about racism requires you to be *present*. And that your cup be relatively full. Like it doesn't have to be running over, but you don't want to be going into that conversation with a half-full cup because your need is going to get in the way of the conversation of you providing the listening that I'm going to describe to you. So the first step is to check in on yourself.

Clarify Your Intention

Amanda:

So, and the other part of checking in with your wise self is checking in with your intention. Like, so before I went back to that neighbor, I was clear about what my intention was. My intention was not to get him to apologize to me or to even make him or her understand where I was coming from. Or have them somehow comfort me or understand me, you know? My intention of that conversation was to apologize and say what I really wanted with them. So, the clearer we are about our intention in these conversations, the better it will go.

The intention that I want to suggest that you have with someone who you have a disagreement with about racism is that you intend to lean in to really understand them and to plant a seed. To just give them a seed of how you look at it.

So, that's the intention that I'm suggesting that you have with someone who you disagree with. You can have other intentions. You can have an intention to hold someone to account. You can have an intention to go off, to just, as they say, "I'm going to speak the truth and shame the devil." You could have that intention, but what I'm going to walk you through though, is if you do decide to lean in and really understand that person, and drop your seed, then I'm going to show you how to do that.

So, I want to be clear, this is not the only intention you could have, but that's the intention I suggest you start off when you're with someone who you disagree with. If you have to protect people—if, for example, you need to shut someone down, like sometimes I'm with teachers, or other folks, facilitators, and if someone is doing harm in their speaking, and what's important is that they stop, then your intention is clear: you shut it down. Like, "Okay, that's not for here, that's not for now." Or whatever your words are to, you know, shut it down.

But this is a really good way to approach someone when you're in a one-on-one situation. This is a really good way to help someone go deeper than the script. That they're not even aware of is really a script. And most of us, and it would be so great if more and more people of European descent were talking with each other about racism in ways like this when people of color aren't around and don't have to do that labor.

I encourage people of color to use these steps but to be aware that you are laboring and to pay careful attention to replenishing your cup.

So, okay, so after you've done that first step, which is to check in with your wise self, make sure that you have relative balance physically, emotionally. And then you set your clear intention, which in this case is to lean in, understand the person better, and to plant your own seed of what you know to be true.

ACTION STEP:

Complete **"Worksheet 1 for Step One: Check in With Your Wise Self Checklist"** below.

Worksheet 1 for Step One: Check in with Your Wise Self Checklist

1. BODY

Does your body need your urgent attention? What parts of your body carry your stress? Are there any tell tale signs that you should not take on a more stressful conversation?

_____

_____

_____

_____

_____

2. EMOTIONS

What are you feeling now— before you have the difficult conversation about racism? What can you do to soothe yourself?

_____

_____

_____

_____

_____

INTENTIONS

Which intention would you consciously choose for this conversation? Is it to listen and learn more? Is it to change their minds and hearts? Is it to practice being present even when you disagree?

_____

_____

_____

_____

_____

Step One when Your Wise Self Says No

Amanda:

Suppose you check in and you notice, "Okay, I'm still hurting from the last conversation I had." So it could be with your kid, your partner, teacher—it doesn't have to have been a conversation about race. But something where you have some hurts. That has you out of balance. Maybe you feel guilty or preoccupied. Your energy is still there or it's being wrapped up there. So when you notice that, what do you do?

Decline the conversation about race or racism and to go take care of yourself. So some people hear that as "decline the conversation about racism." But they're like, "Go take care of myself. What does that mean?" Go play a video game? Go hang out on Facebook? Do some surfing like Erika was talking about, where it's like, "Wow. Half an hour went by? What the hell have I been doing?" I'll just be clear, that is *not* what I mean. 'Cause that is like distracting yourself rather than turning *towards* that thing that has you off balance. So if what you see is that you're hungry or you have to use the bathroom, of course I want you to go use the bathroom or give yourself some food. Don't keep ignoring yourself, in other words. Now if you're imbalanced and if your need is something else, you noticed that—let's say you notice that you're exhausted.

This happened to me yesterday. A friend of mine was giving a talk on queer identities or queer realities in the Caribbean. I really wanted to support her. I got all the way there, hit all this traffic, and I got there, parked, and I just realized, *I'm exhausted.* And from this talk I need to go to this meeting. And I felt like, "I'm out of integrity if I go to this talk this way." This is not how I'm saying I want to live my life and what I'm telling other people to do. Even though I wanted to support her. So I did a couple of short meditations that helped to refresh me, to relax my body, and I didn't get to take a full on nap, but I got to do that. And I noticed—and I just want to check in with you guys—I noticed that part of me, even though I said I can't go to her talk because I'm exhausted, part of me wanted to get on my phone and answer emails. There's a big

42

part of me that did not want to address myself and nurture myself. So I don't want us to take that for granted and I wanted to spend a little bit of time with you on that part of the step. When you disengage to take care of yourself, please follow through and take care of yourself. So I wonder what's rising for you. Thoughts about that? Any experiences.

Debbie:

I've actually just come off an experience where I stepped aside from a leadership role. I felt like I was doing good work, but I also noticed how much it was depleting me, and I had a lot of guilt around stepping aside. Took me a long time to do. And I'm now two weeks out and I'm noticing so much about what I now have the capacity for as a result of giving myself permission to stop the work that was exhausting me. So it is really a big theme for me and informing a lot of the way that I interact with people.

Amanda:

Wow. There's a whole lot in that. Did anybody get my email this morning about who's responsible for Black fragility? We can prevent fragility by turning towards—actively— turning towards the things that actually feed us. Sometimes we have to do things that are pulling a lot out of us. But we also need to actively turning towards that which is filling our cups. And sometimes let go of the thing that's draining you. So I appreciate hearing that. Thank you. Anybody else on taking care of yourself or saying that you want to but never seeming to quite do it?

Sam:

I've been working on a personality trait I have of saying yes to too many things. And over the past three, four years—basically since I retired from my work in the world, my paying work,. I have been doing more of the conversations with white people and education about race and racial issues. That work is really, really important to me. And it's also extremely exhausting and draining. And so, actually, what I found was that it was really important for me to set priorities, to be able to set priorities, and live and let saying no become a spiritual practice. So actually saying, "I know that I said I would serve on this committee. It's not something that I can continue to do. I need to make more space in my life."

And then that space also allows me to actually do things that help me take care of myself—like going to a yoga class, or going to the gym and exercising, or just reading a book for fun, reading a mystery, or things like that. The sort of balance of being able to say no and to know what's really the number one priority, discerning what's really important for me to do.

Amanda:

Here's a phrase that I got from the really amazing Andrea J. Lee, a Chinese Canadian: "No is the bodyguard of yes." By saying no to something, what are you saying yes to? And that might even help with some of the guilt. So you know how on this step, and I'll come to you, Daniel, next. You know how on this step, I'm asking, "Are you exhausted? Are you emotionally imbalanced? Hungry? Are you in a lot of pain?" So if one of the ways that you keep yourself healthy and balanced is by going to the gym or doing yoga, having time to go to market or reading a novel, reading fiction—not just reading books about the suffering and justice. You gotta think about what is the, what is the other stuff you're putting inside yourself? And making time for *that* kind of information to come inside of you.

Jo, another African American client, sent me a link to an article from a white NBA player where he took the stand regarding racial justice and what he stood for. And he ended it by saying, "So if you buy my jersey, know that I stand for this. If you do this, know that I stand for this." He really wanted to say, "This is what my image means when you buy this." And I thanked her and I said, "Wow, that was really moving." And she said, "It gives me hope." And the thing is, what do you want to put inside your consciousness? Don't you want to put stuff in there that gives you *hope*, as well as the pain and the suffering. Okay, Daniel.

Daniel:

I was just reflecting that it seems sort of perverse to me, but the only way that I can consistently do self care is by considering it part of the job. That's just the way I'm made, I guess. That works, but nothing else other than that does.

Amanda:

So when you say you consider it part of a job, tell me what you mean.

Daniel:

It's helped that my wife retired a couple of weeks ago and so she's really pushing me to do this sort of stuff—do the self care kind of thing. If self-care becomes part of my work, the same as making phone calls, doing emails, reading, all of that.then it will be a significant part of my life.

Amanda:

Awesome. Great. If it works, keep with it. Awesome. Yeah, Erika?

Erika:

I resonate with what Daniel said and I put in the chat that phrase that you've used, "You are your instrument of transformation." And I've done hospice chaplaincy and that was absolutely critical and obvious to me for that work. For this work, it's not always as obvious, but just as important.

I wanted to share something that I found really helpful. Not that I can always follow it, but when I find myself really getting hooked into the things that are temptations, like playing little games on my phone, or looking at yarn online or things like that, asking the question, "Are you really *lonely*?" or "What are you really *hungry* for?" Because often those things are like, I'm yearning for something and that's how I'm filling it. And it doesn't work. To turn instead toward, "What is the hunger for? Is it for a kind of connection?" And how do you tend to that compassionately?—is so important.

Amanda:

Wow. Thank you. Yeah, that's all that turning towards it rather than running away from it. Thank you. And in fact it resonates with what we're saying, right? Cause we want to help other people turn towards to be able to see racism, right? Be able to see their part in it. But if we ourselves play the game of I-don't-want-to-see-what-I-don't-want-to-see, and pretend. There's lack of integrity there, right? Cause in your own experience, you're doing what you're telling people they shouldn't do. So, awesome.

When You Say No: Some Practical Ways to Nourish Yourself

Amanda:

The *Black Girl Magic* album can help you to turn toward yourself to process emotions and hurts. The things that I've used are:

  - journaling,

  - talking with the trusted person who has a racial justice lens and a compassion lens,

  - *Feel Flow*, which is on the album. (None of you have used that yet. So maybe I invite you to try that out on one of these breaks.)

  - Ho'oponopono. See the *Black Girl Magic* album.

When there is a whole lot of energy there, a *big* hurt, *it's going to take more time*, and *it may take more than one method*. So I want to encourage you, don't lose faith if you turn towards it, and you journal, and it's still with you. Remember the incident with my neighbor took me a full week.

Talking with a Trusted Person vs. Venting

Amanda:

Also notice I suggest you talk with a trusted person; this is not venting. In our Women of Color Leadership Group we were talking about how venting gets the situation out there, but it doesn't necessarily make you feel better. But talking with a trusted person who knows how to hold space for transformation and hold you to account, can help you to heal and grow.

Role Play: Practice Declining a Conversation about Racism

Now we get to do a role play. And this role play is where you get to practice declining a conversation about racism. Pair with someone and each of you will have a turn. So we'll call one person the White Script Person and we're going to call the other person the Racial Justice Person. The White Script Person will launch into a conversation about racism. The Racial Justice Person, will decline the conversation but to let the White Script Person when you would like to pick it back up. Then you will switch playing the roles so that each of you gets to practice finding the words to decline a conversation.

ACTION STEP:

Complete the second **Worksheet for Step One: "Declining a Conversation"** below.

Worksheet for Step One: Declining a Conversation

1. What feelings or concerns come up inside you when you choose to decline?

_____

_____

2. Do you say yes when you really don't have the capacity? Why?

_____

_____

_____

3. When you don't have the capacity to say yes, how do you nourish yourself?

If you distract yourself, what do you do instead? How could you treat yourself lovingly?

_____

_____

_____

4. Reflections for after declining the conversation.

- Acknowledge yourself for making the effort. Note what you did well or how you might have stretched yourself. Find something positive to affirm about yourself.

_____

_____

- Ask yourself: what would help you to consciously accept or decline the next conversation about racism?

_____

_____

What Comes up for You when You Decline?

Amanda:

Let's see what happened when you said no.

Debbie:

Declining the conversation about race but not walking away from the interaction because I needed something else from it. We were having a relaxing after-work drink and I had wanted to chat.

Amanda:

Okay. That's interesting. Making that distinction. Like, okay, "I don't want to talk with you about racism right now, so let's come back to this." So this moment. Yeah, and that's honest.

Sam:

I found it useful to have the other person say something was going on with them. 'I'm feeling tired right now and this deserves my attention and said I just can't talk about that right now.'

Amanda:

 So giving somebody a little bit of insight to how you're feeling and why you're declining right now. Erika?

Erika:

"I'm feeling a bit distracted. I'm not in the right headspace right now." That idea, "It's not you, it's me."

Amanda:

Right.

Erika:

The vulnerability is connecting.

Amanda:

Right. And I even like that phrase, Erika: "It's not you, it's me. I just can't do this right now." "I'm so tired, but I do want to talk about it."

Daniel:

Well, this came up in the sharing about what we would do to the self-care part. Part of it would be simply continuing a conversation with a person after having set up the time to talk about racism. Continuing to build a relationship.

Amanda:

Gotcha. Okay, good. Did you want to add more, Debbie?

Debbie:

This is a regular experience for me because I often meet with a group of 10 to 12 white women who are politically in very different places, and we kind of have a practice of saying, okay this got too hot. Cause our priority is taking care of each other and so this is a common practice. "Okay. We're trying to do too much here," because we don't want to break up the opportunity to nourish each other.

Amanda:

Wow. I think that there's a couple things I would say about that. One is that Niyonu Spann, who is a mentor for me, she always says, "Know what it is that you're up to." Know what it is that you're up to. So what is this group up to? What are we agreeing to in this moment? So that's awesome to have that clarity. And I just feel like I want to say this—I don't know that it needs to be said to you four, but maybe somebody else on the call needs to hear this:

I was thinking the other day about how many relationships I've had, how uncomfortable I have felt when white women call me "sister"—on the basis of gender, when I haven't seen them stand for racial justice. And so that thing about focusing on nourishing the relationship, nourishing the bond—I think it's an *and*, maybe it's a polarity—nourishing the bond *and* being able to bring difficult stuff to the relationship, which can of course strengthen the bond. But also stretches and tenses. So, well, I'm going to leave that one right there for the moment.

STEP TWO: HOLD SPACE FOR TRANSFORMATION

Amanda:

The second step is to Hold Space for Transformation.

So, I go into great detail about this in my master class, and I offer free recordings, so I'm going to be brief here and just have us walk through it. So, Holding Space for Transformation is setting an intention to be unconditional love and unconditional acceptance. That's how Niyonu Spann defines it, and she's the person who first introduced it to me. And what I've found is that some of us have a hard time tapping in, to *being* unconditional love and unconditional acceptance. Like, those words don't mean a lot to us, or they feel really scary to us, like somehow we're going to lose the ground of justice. So, what I suggest is that you get practical with it. You get your feet on the ground. If you're sitting, you feel your butt in the chair. And once you get yourself into your physical body, then you turn to your breath.

And I like to breathe directly into my heart center.

And then I say a phrase that further helps me get there. I say to myself silently, "I am unconditional love. I am unconditional acceptance."

ACTION STEP:

Follow along as Amanda leads Holding Space in this recording.

So, if you want to try this with me, maybe putting one of your hands or both of your hands on your heart center, breathing in unconditional love, breathing in unconditional acceptance. Some people like to use other phrases. One woman, who I'm working with now, she says, "Breathing in love, breathing out hate, breathing in peace, breathing out fear." So you just have to find a touchstone phrase that really makes you feel safe, connected, and like big, you know? Or like a speck that's connected to something really huge, something bigger than your ego.

I'm going to give you a moment. Awesome. So, if your eyes have been closed, go ahead and open them, maybe wiggle your fingers, your toes. I like to rub my hands together just to give myself some of that beautiful energy that I just generated.

Imagine, if you could take that feeling that you have right now into a conversation about racism.

Suppose you generated that before you started the conversation, or suppose you remind yourself to get your feet on the ground and find your breath when you find yourself. Or in the middle of a conversation. What would that be like?

I want you to know that, maybe it could sound a little too easy, or maybe it sounds like a little too loving, or a little too generous to some people who you think are, you know, various epithets. And what I want you to know is that this is a way to sustain *you*, so that you can stay in this beyond the sprint—for the long term. Holding space can be especially liberating for people of color. For example, one Indian Amerian woman shared that holding space allowed her to have a conversation about white fragility with two strangers on an airplane. And another used it to help recover from the damaging impact of her previous work environment, where she was the only African American in management. So she was using it as a way to bring some healing back to herself. Just the other day another woman sent me an email with the subject headline "It works." Checking in with her wise self and holding space for transformation had restored her power in her conversations with white colleagues.

So, it sets you up to shift your listening so you become a better listener, but it also sets you up to connect with God, your ancestors, your higher self, or whatever you choose to rely on other than your ego.

Please take a break to drink some water and do some form of self-care. Follow this link amandakemp.bandcamp.com to my *Black Girl Magic* album to listen to a guided meditation. It could be Hold Space for Transformation, it could be a Loving-kindness meditation, or it could be the Black Girl Body Scan. If you're not a Black girl, that's okay. You can still do this, it's still going to be good for you. But, if you have another form of self-care that you like to use, go ahead and use it.

ACTION STEP:

Do one self-care practice from the *Black Girl Magic* album.

STEP TWO: HOLD SPACE FOR TRANSFORMATION (continued)

Amanda:

All right, welcome back everybody. In this next bit of time, we're going to focus on Holding Space for Transformation, which is Step Two. And I want to share a slide with you so you have it all in one place. What are the steps to Holding Space for Transformation?

So as you can see, in Holding Space for Transformation, when we say Step Two, when you have achieved some kind of balance and you feel like you're ready or you're willing to have this conversation, then here's a quick checklist.

- Get both your feet on the ground, or feel the ground underneath you.

- Get into your breath.

- Open your heart.

- And then finally silently or quietly repeat your phrase. And like I said, my phrase is "unconditional love and unconditional acceptance." If there's another phrase that works for you. Some people I've heard use touchstone phrases like, "Your will, Your will Lord." I've heard people say, "Thy will be done." or "Lord, make me an instrument of your peace." "I'm willing." So it's whatever phrase that gets you to that very connected space of being connected to something way, way bigger than yourself that infuses you with love, that infuses *you* with love and unconditional acceptance.

So one thing you might be wondering is, how will you do all that when you know you've got somebody sitting right in front of you, who's already kicked off the conversation? And so we're going to get a chance to practice.

Holding Space *while* in a Difficult Conversation

Amanda:

So how do you hold space in the middle of a conversation? When I feel myself tense in a conversation, I start Holding Space. When I exploded a week ago, I didn't sense anything. I just kind of blew. But generally I have a telltale sign. Something starts to tense up and so I have to make that determination internally. "Am I going to do this right now?" And if I'm a yes, then I get my feet on the ground, and I really focus on breathing. I'm listening, but I'm really focused, even more than I'm listening to you, I'm focusing on *me*, on *tuning* me with the breath, and getting to my heart.

And the second thing I want to say about this is: Don't be afraid to pause. To have someone *else* pause while you get yourself there. Keep checking in to make sure that you are present. If you notice that you've exited, or that part of you isn't present, then you can pause the person. Just say, "I need a breath." And the breath is a bridge to coming back into your body, into that moment, into knowing. Check in to see what you need to stay present or if you need to leave. You might find out: "Wow, I can't do any more." Or "Okay, I can do this." "I need some water, but I'm good," or "I need to use the bathroom, but I'm good."

Whatever it is. It's like the breath is another moment where you could check in with yourself. So let's do a demo for the whole group, and then let's break it apart together.

Holding Space while in a Difficult Conversation (Role Play)

Amanda:

So let's do a demo for the whole group and then let's break it apart together. So Erika, maybe you should just be my partner in this, and I'm going to take the easy part, Erika.

Erika:

Okay.

Amanda:

I'm going to be the White Script Person and you be the Racial Justice Person. And you practice Holding.

Erika:

Okay.

Amanda:

Let's start. Hey, Erika.

Erika:

Hey, how are you, Amanda?

Amanda:

I'm good, I'm good. You know, something happened? I know you follow a lot race issues 'cause I see your posts or Facebook and you making announcements a lot at church about this kind of stuff. So I was wondering, what you think about Jussie, what's his name? Smollett? The guy who pretended that he got beat up and wasted the police's time. And there's all this tension in Chicago and now the DA doesn't want to prosecute him, but the police union is mad at her, and I don't blame them. I think that he shouldn't...We shouldn't be going through this. People shouldn't use racism frivolously. And I just feel like he's... It's just a mess. It's just a mess out there.

Erika:

Mm hmm. Yeah, I hear you...Yes. Really emotional stuff.

Amanda:

It just makes me sick inside my heart. Why can't we just all get along? Why can't people know? We're just people, for God's sake! We're just people.

Erika:

You know, when you say, " Why can't we all get along?" I hear you yearning for, or being frustrated, but also yearning for connection. Can you tell me more? What are some of the things that go on when you hear this? What do you feel?

Amanda:

Well, I just feel...I feel scared. And I feel lonely.

Erika:

Yeah.

Amanda:

I just want to live somewhere else. Or I want to make this a good place again.

Erika:

Yeah, me too. I hear you.

Amanda:

So, let's pause. Great. Thank you. Let's check in about what that was like. Erika, what was that like for you?

Erika:

So I noticed in myself this momentary thought, "You know they came back and corrected that." And I know that's

not where you go, you know? So...

Amanda:

Erika, you reined in your desire to correct my facts. You caught it.

Erika:

Yeah. I was really aware of needing to stay with my breath and trying to listen underneath for some of the feelings

and just ask about them. And I'm not sure how many people would confess that they're scared, but if you

get to that point, wow, that just felt like here's a place of connection. This, I can resonate to and if

somebody can get to here, we've got such common ground to work with, you know? So by the time I say,

"I feel you," that's real. I really do. And somebody saying I want to make this better. I'm like, "Yeah!"

Anything else that you would want to hear about what it feels like on this side?

Sam:

So this is actually more a comment than a question, but I noticed that there was at least one time where you really

took a moment to take in what Amanda was saying and one time you even closed your eyes. And I was just

going, "Wow, I wonder what she's doing there?" And it ended up good. But I wonder how it felt to you,

Amanda, when she closed her eyes like that?

Amanda:

Yeah, good question. It was a memorable moment for me too, and I really felt like she was listening. I felt like she

was zooming in. But sometimes I felt like, you could've used fewer words, Erika. Because when I felt you *feeling*, I was more inclined to share. You actually didn't need to ask me for more about those feelings, you know? Because I was upset, I was willing to just say it. So nodding, "mmm," "yeah"and *meaning* it—really does help. As you saw, I got to a space of, "Well, I feel scared." I got to that space anyway.

Erika:

The nonverbals are just as important.

Amanda:

Yes. Don't worry about what you have to say to draw me out. Silence can often draw people out.

Erika:

Yes.

Amanda:

And you're really looking and listening. I felt listened to. Even though I asked questions like "I don't know how you feel, Erika? or "I wonder what you think, Erika?" what I really wanted was to tell you what I thought because I know you care about these issues." So be aware of that too. When people say, "I don't know what you think" or "I wonder what you think," they may not actually be ready to hear it yet.

Well then let's practice it again. So in your pair, decide which one is going to be the Racial Justice Person in which one is going to be working with the white script. And all you have to do is Hold Space for Transformation. And remember non-verbals. We're only working on Steps One and Two right now. So just get yourself to transition. So we're working on the transition from someone's "blah, blah, blah" to racism. You're like, "Okay, now I gotta Hold Space." So how you make that transition. Okay. And get yourself grounded and Holding Space for Transformation.

Triggers that Get in the Way of Holding Space for Transformation

Amanda:

Before we move on to Step Three, which is to Lean In, let's talk about our triggers and how we can work on neutralizing them or understanding them, so that we can stay present even when the person says something that we really can't stand. The goal is to have fewer and fewer things that trigger us as we move forward.

ACTION STEP:

Complete the exercise "**Neutralizing Triggers**" below.

Exercise: Neutralizing Triggers

1. Find a buddy to practice with. If you don't have one, request one among those in our private Facebook group, "Transform Your Conversations about Racism."

2. Find a phrase or sentence on the topic of race that really pushes your buttons.

3. Have your buddy say that phrase or sentence to you while you practice Holding Space for Transformation.

4. Pause and repeat twice more.

5. Reflect to your partner: What was this like? Did you notice any changes from the first to the third

  time?

_____

_____

_____

6. Switch partners and repeat the exercise.

7. Please share your observations in your journal.

_____

_____

_____

Triggers that Get in the Way of Holding Space for Transformation (continued)

Amanda:

Okay so you had a chance to hear your trigger at least twice, maybe three times from your partner, and to digest it.

So, who would like to share what opened up for you in doing that? Yeah, Debbie.

Debbie:

So, Erika said my trigger and actually, I got a little teary. It was, I hadn't realized just how raw it is to me and it's very specific. I think generally I don't have that many, but that particular one, is very, very common where I am, and it's making me very angry. So it was hard to calm down, it went right up to an eight or nine. And we talked for a little while and then, when she said my trigger again, I decided to laugh, which for me is a physical thing. I know I'm going to have to come back to this because this is my work. But at least I can manage here to assume that the person is well-intentioned enough that I don't need to be angry, or run screaming from the room, because I gotta do this work.

Amanda:

You noticed your physiological reactions each time, and it seems like when you said that the laughter came second. If it was an eight or a nine to start with, when you laughed was it still at an eight or nine?

Debbie:

I think it's still pretty raw for me, and it's hard to just let go, that particular one.

Amanda:

Yeah.

Debbie:

I'm not quite ready to let go. I'm still grieving.

Amanda:

Oh, yeah.

Debbie:

And so laughter is *instead* of crying, rather than saying, "I don't have to attach to this." I think it's too hard still.

Amanda:

Gotcha, okay. Good. Thank you, Debbie, thank you. Appreciate it.

Amanda:

Anybody else want to share what showed up for you? What you're learning, processing about yourself?

Sam:

Well, it was a little hard, because we've been doing this work all day, and because I knew what was coming. I don't think the statement was as triggering as it would be in real life. So what normally might drive me up to a seven or eight was probably more like a six or a five. There was a decrease with repeating it. But I think it probably still would be pretty triggering in a conversation, if people just said that.

Amanda:

Yeah, great. Thank you.

Amanda:

Great, do you want to share what it was like for you, Daniel?

Daniel:

Hearing racist stuff doesn't trigger me—to the extent that I am in touch with my feelings—I don't have the sense that I'm triggered by stuff.

Amanda:

Okay. Well that's good. I mean, if the point is that what you uncovered is that not much triggers you, then that's okay. It's not like you have to have triggers. What I would point you to, Daniel, is—and this is for anybody else who doesn't have a lot of emotional stuff readily available to them—then I would rephrase it as, "What makes you want to turn away?"

Daniel:

Yeah, there are things like that that I don't respond to by getting angry, but pulling away is something that does happen, yes.

Amanda:

Yeah, so I'm glad you brought your experience up because I'm sure there are people, lots of people like that. And there are, those of us on the call, who do both, who have a pull away for some actions, and then, kind of like a fire or tears for something else.

Awesome, did you want to add anything Erika?

Erika:

My trigger phrase was, "Why do you have to make this about race?" When I heard it, I was questioning myself, "Are they right? Am I imposing something? Is this my agenda?" Because I have a history of being the smart kid in the class, and being too much of a showoff and being told, "You're taking up too much space." So that's what gets triggered for me. And then I start feeling deeply, personally criticized rather than curious about the question: "Is this about racism or not?"

Amanda:

You know, I really appreciate you bringing that up, because sometimes conversations about racism are a surrogate for another conversation. So Robin DiAngelo says it can be a surrogate for, "Am I a good or bad person?" So we keep talking about affirmative action, we keep talking about school achievement but really, what I'm really debating, and even unknown to myself, is, "Am I good or am I bad?" And for a lot of us it's, "Am I bad?" more so than, "Am I good?" that we're working on.

I want to take a breath, because this is a choice point for me in terms of where we go.

So, Erika since you brought this up, and you were able to identify a core self-doubt that you're working with, is there something that you could say to yourself afterwards, or in the middle of, that would *soothe* that part of you, that would help you to Lean In to hear the other person?

Erika:

I think it's really helpful to just *recognize*, like "Wow, this touches something really young." To be tender and just to recognize that's part of what's going on. That feels useful, because I think otherwise it's just kind of asserting itself.

Amanda:

So, I think when Erika said "a young part of herself" and "to recognize this,"—that that's happening, that it's activated, is important. Yeah, I agree. That's like, who knows, maybe that's even 70% of it, is just being able to see it, feel it.

Erika:

I think it being "young" allows me to be compassionate for it; to say, "it's okay, baby," or, "it's okay to feel like you want to cry," or whatever. Yeah, Sam, says in the chat, "Good time to Hold Space for yourself."

Yeah, definitely. Definitely. Just breathing I think is a way to take a step into the inner sanctum.

Amanda:

Yeah, and if you know that this is a hard, you know this is a tender core thing for you, then I encourage you to use the self-compassion tools that we have to *be* with it, to be accepting of it. And I'm just thinking about what you have access to, but I won't try to be specific about which tool that everyone can use from the public, but use something that helps you to recognize that it hurts, and show yourself sympathy.

Thank you, and that whole thing about "it's okay, baby," and giving yourself that kindness, is so huge. Because when you give it to yourself, then you're not asking the other person in the conversation to extend it to you, which they may or may not have the capacity to do, or even the knowledge of that's what they just activated.

So, yeah this is why doing this kind of trigger work is really powerful. To your point, Sam, when you said the phrase that you said that today your trigger phrase was only a five or six when it might normally be a seven or eight that's because of the work we've been doing, prior to the moment that you started the exercise. We've been practicing a lot of self-acceptance, self care, compassionate listening, being in a compassionate circle.

Yeah, so we have a whole worksheet on feelings and beliefs, so we're not going to go more in depth on this training with that, but getting in touch with what is the belief that this triggering statement is causing over here in you—being a toxic belief that you have about yourself, something you haven't forgiven yourself for—that you uncover the belief and not even to debate it but just, as Erika was saying, to uncover it, to be with it, and to be in sympathy with yourself...That this is *hard*. Walking around with this belief or this hurt about myself is hard. And seeing what happens. Again, if you were part of our community and have these chances for a conversation like this, a one-on-one, then we could work it through, but there are other ways that you could do it on your own, too.

I just want to give a moment of breath. (Pause.)

Let's just imagine the person who's just giving you the script, but then what they've really got going on is another hurt or belief about themselves that they're arguing against. And by you Holding Space, by you not engaging in the argument of they're wrong or they're right, people sometimes turn themselves around. They'll talk and talk and then they'll go, "I don't know what I'm saying, Amanda. What the hell, I hear the contradictions myself," or, "Maybe this is white fragility that's coming out of my mouth right now." Both those things have literally been said to me by white people I've been in conversation with. So sometimes people can see things that they can't see if you engage them on the level of the topic.

STEP THREE: LEAN IN

Amanda:

So let's get to how to Lean In.

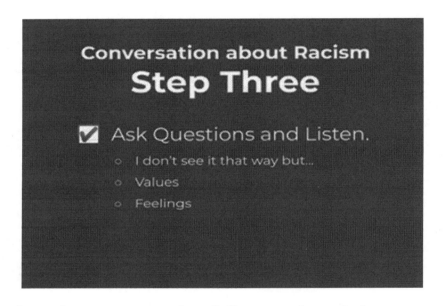

Okay, so Step Three: ask questions, try to get to values, feelings, to understand why.

So I want to talk about this a little bit because this tends to be where things fall apart.

Earlier, Erika said she put the person on the defensive by correcting her facts about quotas, and the rest of the conversation was all about arguing something. Maybe it was about arguing their goodness, their intelligence, their worthiness. So when you say "I don't see it that way"—there's a *bit* of a charge to it, but it doesn't have to be a *big* charge. It depends on how we say it, and so on that other person's side, "I don't see it that way, but I'd like to hear from you. I'd like to understand why you do." "Would you be willing to share with me a little bit more about it—why you see it that way?"

So why are we advocating this?

I think I've already said a few things about how we know what changes people's minds is not you disagreeing with them and giving them more facts. But let's talk a little bit more about the nervous system.

If you choose to directly challenge someone, a lot of the time you will trigger their flight or their fight response. So, Debbie, you said earlier that you squish people; your fight mode squishes people, so that's like a flight response. People shut down, they pull away from you—energetically if not physically. And then some people will just fight till the end, and Erika gave an example of that. There was just no going deep, that conversation was just going to stay a fight.

When we step into unconditional love and unconditional acceptance, we tone down our own flight and fight activation which, because people tend to mirror each other, can help to also lower someone else's fight or flight.

Also when we give people *space,* they can see things that they may not normally be able to see. But when we don't, when we view them as an enemy rather than an opponent in this situation, then that affects how we talk and our ways of being which people react to. People know.   People have a sense of when they're being lied to, when they're being condescended to, and when they're being implicitly told that they're stupid.

Mindset Shifts:

Opponents Rather than Enemies

Amanda:

Ricardo Levins Morales introduced me to some mindset shifts that I've found helpful in conflicts. If you adopt them, you can lean in without correcting and overpowering. First, view the person in front of you as an opponent not your *enemy. You might agree on something else* but "on this issue we're *disagreeing.*"

Photo CC 2013 by Edwin Martinez

Take the example of Venus and Serena. We know they disagree when they're on the court in singles competition. Did you see the U.S. open when they faced each other? It was over pretty quick because Serena showed no mercy. She was like "bam, bam, bam!" Serena showed no mercy. And Venus did her best. She wasn't trying to take it easy on her sister, either. She wanted to advance. But in the end when Serena won, she honored her sister, because despite that, they're still sisters. So try looking at the people we're disagreeing with as not enemies but as opponents who could grow. In contrast, when we view someone as an enemy our stress levels and sense of kill or be killed is high.

Tunnels Rather than Bridges

Of course Ricardo's not the first person to suggest that we look at people as opponents rather than enemies. You could say that was Dr. King and Jesus's teaching too. Ricardo is just a little closer since he's a Puerto Rican who lives and organizes in Minneapolis. Ricardo also says he doesn't believe in building bridges with people. Instead, *tunnel down* to where you actually *already* have common ground, to where you actually already have unity."

I interpret that to mean go beneath the surface to really listen for and hear the opponent's *why*, what's motivating them.

For example, let's say a European American said "My family worked really hard, I feel like this policy is is punishing people who worked really hard for what they have." You could tunnel down beneath that to shared agreement. "You think that when people work hard, they should see the benefit of their hard work."

The point is that when you're listening deeper, you're listening for common ground. You don't even have to say, "I agree with this," but if you can touch on that agreement, it affects how you are with the person, all before you speak.

Why This Works

Let's review why Leaning In works.

- It moves them and you out of fight and flight.

- It also moves you into a stance of wanting to open and connect. By open and connect I don't just mean to that person but I also mean to something higher, that could be to your God, the values that you're committed to living by, your ancestors, etc.

- It helps you to be the change you want to see. Niyonu Spann, a giant in the field of Diversity, Equity and Inclusion, often uses a Goethe quote in her trainings: "To create that thing you must be that thing." I like to think of it as "to see something bear fruit, to see kindness or to see inclusion or to see justice, compassion, beloved community, you've gotta *be* that." And how you're *being* in this conversation, is you planting a new seed for that new society that you want to see, or that new kind of relationship, or new way of handling power, or a new way of handling your masculinity or your femininity.

So when we say we're Holding Space for Transformation, we're not just Holding Space for the other person to change their mind. We're Holding Space for that bigger thing that we're committed to.

In the example I gave you about my neighbor, I apologized and I also said, I really want to be a good neighbor. I knew that's what I was committed to. I also, as Erika knows, I'm committed to staying grounded, staying compassionate, et cetera. So I can't get good neighbors and good neighborliness in my community without me being willing to practice it. I can't get there without watering the seeds in me that have that potential.

So when I say in Step Three to say, "I don't see it that way, but..." or "I look at it differently, and..." we want you to be honest, if it's true that you do see it differently, or you don't see it that way. So we're not buttering people up, coming back to the technique Daniel was talking about earlier. But we are staying *present*. We're not pulling away from them emotionally. We're leaning *in*, in fact. So let's take a break.

ACTION STEP:

Complete **"Worksheet 1 for Step Three: Leaning In"** below.

Worksheet 1 for Step Three: Leaning In

1. Have you ever been thanked for listening to someone well? What did you do? What did you not do?

_____

_____

_____

2. What's the difference between using silence as a weapon and using silence to absorb someone's truth?

_____

_____

_____

3. How do you get yourself connected to your heart?

_____

_____

_____

4. Think of a time when you chose to connect with someone that you did not like or agree with. Why did you choose to connect? What did you have to change about yourself?

_____

_____

_____

5. What kinds of questions make you feel defensive?

_____

_____

_____

6. What kinds of questions make you want to share more deeply?

_____

_____

_____

7. How is "leaning in" different than simply agreeing with someone?

_____

_____

_____

Mindset Shift: "They are you."

Amanda:

Now this might be advanced, but let me put it out here. Everybody on this call has a statement that triggers us. So, in addition to neutralizing the trigger by our earlier practice of repetition and being present to our feelings, I want to offer another option. That is to give the triggering statement some space. Write from the perspective of the part of you that feels that way. We want to listen to that voice, give it some space, without condemning it—even though we know it's not true. But being with that voice, being with those voices *in you* helps to make it less of a trigger when it comes at you from somewhere else.

And the reason I'm saying this is, I debated saying this earlier and I wasn't going to go here, but I think you're ready. If it's showing up in your world as a statement that really gets you going, then it's living in you somewhere. I'm suggesting that something is mirroring something inside you.. And so the way to deal with it isn't to get rid of the person, or to pull away from that person, but to face it in you. To talk with it in you. To befriend it, to just give it some love and attention and see what is underneath that thing.

So let's have some feedback. Remember, take what you like and leave the rest. So, yeah, Debbie.

Debbie:

I think that one of the things that you're—I'm really thinking about your suggestion and it's deep work so I won't share all of that, but—I think that when something brings up shame, that's quite a hard one. What I'm recognizing is that when I'm triggered, people are touching a very deep sense of shame in me that I have failed to right the wrongs in the world. I hate that I live in a society that hasn't addressed this problem, and I feel very guilty about that. The dangerous part is when you start feeling shame yourself, it really makes you want to shame somebody else, and that's the dark place that you get into.

What you said is really helpful, and it takes a little work to get to what is the thing.

Amanda:

Yeah, wow. I just want to give an amen to that. When we feel shame about something, ooh, it's true. We want to push that off on somebody else. I *agree*. In my limited experience, I have done it, so I'm just saying...Go ahead, Sam.

Sam:

I just want to say, Debbie, how much I resonate with that and my experience is that when I first started, even very long ago, realizing what has really happened in this country around race, racism, slavery, the whole thing—how can you be a white person and not feel shame and guilt about that? I realize that it's a normal reaction for people to feel shame and guilt. And then when people say to me, "Why do you want me to feel guilty and ashamed?" I realize I need to step back and say, "Wow, you know that really hurts, because I know what it's like."

But it's so hard. And no good work can come from that place of shame and guilt. I really feel like the only thing that's helped me is staying with this stuff long enough to find the good "why" to do this work: not because I'm ashamed and I feel guilty that I haven't fixed the world, but because I love myself and I love the world and I want this world to be a better place. And then we'll all be liberated. So it's more collective liberation that is my goal.

Amanda:

Sam, you brought up a good point when you said that somebody accused you of trying to make them feel guilty or ashamed. I'm sure lots of us have heard something along that flavor, right? Sam, I'm wondering if what they're reacting to is the guilt that was already there, and they're projecting it back out to you. That's one way to look at that. Thank you. I hadn't really thought about that before..

ACTION STEP:

Use **"Worksheet 2 for Step Three"** below to practice Steps 1-3. Focus on listening for values, hurts, and common ground.

Worksheet 2 for Step Three: Listen for Values, Hurts, and Common Ground

This course is experiential. Your experience is a great teacher. Find out what happens when you actually practice this step.

1. Find a buddy to practice with. If you don't have one, request one among those in our private Facebook group, "Transform Your Conversations about Racism."

2. Create a role play where they approach you to talk about racism. Set a timer for 3-5 minutes. Let them speak about racism using ideas from the white script. Go through steps 1-3. You're going to:

   • Say yes to the conversation.

   • Hold Space for Transformation.

   • LISTEN. Really listen—for values, for their why, or the common ground underneath it all. You might even listen for, "Is there a hurt in here?" Sometimes when there's a lot of emotion coming from somebody, there's a hurt there.

STEP THREE: LEAN IN

Take enough time so that your buddy really feels heard—to the point where they feel like, either, "I have nothing else to say," or "Wow, I really do want to hear from you."

3. Thank your buddy. Ask them to share when or if they felt listened to. Share what it was like for you to listen in that way.

4. Please journal about your experience.

_____

_____

_____

_____

Reflecting on Step Three Practice

Amanda:

I would love to hear if there are any ah-ha's. What has opened up for you?

Debbie:

It was very useful for me to notice how *quickly* I wanted to engage Sam in the discussion. I was trying to move to

Step 4. I did not easily spend time just listening to her explore her own shame. I quickly wanted to move on.

I was nice about it, but it was hard to stay with, "Tell me more."

Amanda:

Yes, Daniel.

Daniel:

I mean there seems to be a limit to the common ground thing. I could do that and look for values, but it was very

hard. There came a point when it seemed helpful to challenge my partner in our practice role play. I guess

the other thing is I need to get better at eye contact, because she felt like I wasn't hearing her, and we were

both in our heads.

Amanda:

Let me just take a breath.

Two things struck me. One is that if you don't drop down to a heart level, then it's very hard for your listening to

encourage someone else to drop down there, because we mirror each other. One of the fruitful things that

you might journal about, Daniel, is "How does staying in my head keep me safe?" That came to me just

now, as a possible opportunity for you.

Erika:

So one of the things that Daniel asked me about in our role play was really helpful. He said, "What is it that I'm looking for in spiritual community?" So I started to talk about safety and peace, and "I want my little snuggle cocoon and nobody to mess it up" (laughs).

And so one of his challenges to me was well, you know, I value those things too, but I think we also look at spiritual growth as important as well. Maybe it's just because I agree with him that I was, like, "! Yeah, right, it is!" So, challenge was helpful intellectually, but it did keep me at the level of intellect.

I was also thinking that we weren't making that much eye contact. That probably let me off the hook. And so I *wasn't* challenged in another way to really be responsive to his concern. Eye contact is part of the open-hearted way that we can challenge people to be real, to invite them to show up with more than their boxing gloves.

Amanda:

Thank you. Hmm. Okay. I want to address the challenge that Daniel made What I want to say is, the level at which you make the intervention can affect what you get. So if you make the intervention at an intellectual level, then you will probably get a response at an intellectual level. That's on the one hand. But it may not even be the words that you ask, so much as where you're coming from.

How Long Do I Lean In?

Amanda:

Okay, for Sam and Debbie, you felt like you didn't reach the point of where the speaker had felt like she had said enough, and she was like, "all right, I need some feedback here"? And let me stay with you guys for a moment Sam and Debbie. Sam, what were the kinds of questions, if any, you were asking Debbie?

Sam:

I was actually the speaker.

Amanda:

Oh, okay.

Sam:

I was being the white script and at a point, we just sort of said, "Oh, let's stop now."

Amanda:

Oh, interesting. At a point you said, "Let's stop now." Why did you say that? Yeah, Debbie.

Debbie:

I realized that I had lost track of what I was trying to do and I felt as though I had gone down a path that was not what I wanted. And I felt like "I'm not doing it here." And I sort of needed to just stop, because I couldn't get it back. And then we had a helpful conversation.

Amanda:

Good. You know, if that should happen in real life, if you get going with somebody and you're like, "Oh, what the heck am I doing?" You have a couple of options. One is, you can pause. You could say, "You know what, I feel like I don't know what I'm doing. I apologize. I'm not really listening well to you. Can we start again?" Or "Can we come back to this another time?" Because maybe something happened, and you sort of split, or you've run out of time.

Be transparent and tell on yourself because in some ways that interrupts the script, right? When you get authentic and you say, "Oh, my God, I'm not even listening to you." you take the train off the predictable track. And then all of a sudden they're like, "Oh, my gosh, you're over there." You're not just preparing your argument. So I think that's good, Debbie, that you said, "Okay, time out, I'm just not sure what I'm doing anymore." Okay.

And the second thing I want to say is: You may not do a lot of talking. I really want you to consider silence doing a lot of the work for you. Okay, you guys both, Debbie and Sam are laughing. What are you guys laughing about?

Sam:

We both talked a lot. And I think we got into one of the reasons that it wasn't really working is that we were in a very intellectual space, so we were just talking at each other. Not just *at* each other, but just talking, and not delving sort of deeper. I laugh at the silence because hey, you know, I'm a Quaker, I'm pretty good at silence, but I don't know if Debbie has that tradition that lets her be more comfortable with silence.

Amanda:

Debbie?

Debbie:

No, almost the opposite. I practice silence for my own spiritual practice, but I'm the youngest of four children by a long way, and so my practice is to keep on trying to get a word in edgewise. My whole style, and I'm really good at telling stories and engaging people, so 15 minutes can go by and you won't realize that you haven't had a chance to speak. It's absolutely my style, so I was laughing because I'm like, "There I go again!" If anybody just wants someone to freewheel chat, I could go on. So I'm trying really hard to practice brevity and I didn't quite manage it there.

Amanda:

And what this shows us is that even though you had an assignment, your go-to, your default is deeply engraved, right? And so to lean in is countercultural for you.

Debbie:

Yes, that's right.

Amanda:

Leaning in goes against your personal style and it's also countercultural. It's not what people expect.

Debbie:

I think as far as white people go, sure. As far as my British culture, actually it's out of my culture and I was a much more chatty girl in a place where a girl shouldn't be heard. But I'm good with it. It's my strength. I speak for a living, people like that. It's my greatest strength and my greatest weakness.

Amanda:

Yes, yes, yes, I got you. Thank you for making that distinction. Now let's practice Leaning In without words.

ACTION STEP:

Complete **"Worksheet 3 for Step Three: Leaning In without Words"** below.

Worksheet 3 for Step Three: Leaning In without Words

With a buddy, practice Leaning In using words as little as possible.

1. Ask your buddy to share with you something from the white script about racism. Set a timer and let the person speak for 2-3 minutes.

2. Consciously say as little as you can. Really focus on being present without asking or talking. Let your eyes ask; let your body language ask. Let the universe do some asking. If you feel yourself tense up, consciously roll the shoulders back, lift up the heart, let the universe do some of the work.

3. After the time is up, ask your buddy what that was like for them. Share what it was like for you.

Reflecting on Leaning In without Words

How do you actively listen and be there for somebody and invite the Spirit to be there, *without using your words?* I think there's a value to that practice. So, let's come back to Debbie and Sam. I think it might be useful for one of you to do a role play with me, and for all of us to watch it, and then to comment on what you're noticing. So, here's what I'm going to ask you to do. Who would be willing to do the role play? (Debbie gestures). Okay, Debbie. So, let's use you for this role play.

So, then Sam, Erika, and Daniel, will you guys actively Hold Space for us? That would be awesome. So, you don't have to make eye contact, Daniel because we're not going to be lookin' at you anyway. But actively hold space for us. So, Debbie,who would you like to be in this situation?

Debbie:

I think that I need the most work on Leaning In. So, you be the White Script Person.

Amanda:

Okay. Let's start the role play.

Debbie:

So, tell me what's on your mind.

Amanda:

So, I've been thinking a lot about this emphasis on why this group is so white. And on the one hand, I really feel like, "Yeah, diversity's good." But on the other hand, I feel like, "That's just beating ourselves up about it; it's getting us nowhere." And I feel like we need to do what we do best, and then the people who want to do it with us will be attracted to us. And this browbeating about why we're so white, and we're so white—it's getting us nowhere.

So, and I know you're one of the people who talks about diversity, Debbie. So, I just wanted to say that to you. I feel like I kinda think, "Well, would you just give it a rest?" Can't we focus on something positive, here?

Debbie:

When you're thinking about what we do best, what does that bring up for you? What are you thinking of?

Amanda:

Well, I'm thinking we're really good at supporting women who are in business for themselves. We're good at giving emotional support to each other. We're, I feel like, we're good at being sisters, mentors, and helpers to each other.

Debbie:

Helpers to each other in the group?

Amanda:

Yeah.

Debbie:

Mm-hmm (affirmative).

Amanda:

And I felt a little scared just when I said that to you, when you were asking what do I think we do best. All of a sudden, I got a little scared, 'cause I was like, "Oh, best." But I think that's why I'm doing this group, is because I wanted that support. And I...there's just so much tension in my life, I just want there to be a space for me.

Debbie:

Right.

Amanda:

You get what I'm saying.

Debbie:

Are you feeling scared right now?

Amanda:

No, I feel a little better since you smiled.

Debbie:

(Laughs)

Amanda:

I just want us to be friends. I just want to be friends, I feel like I have to work so hard everywhere in my life. Can I

just not work hard here?

Debbie:

Tell me more about what you need from the group.

Amanda:

I think my needs are getting met in the group. I feel like I have friends, I know how to do it. I'm pretty happy with

the group.

Debbie:

Mm-hmm (affirmative). So, what was it that came up for you? Something was going wrong for you when you

started talking. Can you talk about where that came up?

Amanda:

Yeah.

Debbie:

What caused that feeling?

Amanda:

There's just all this pressure —that if we don't get diverse, then somehow we're bad people, or our organization is a

piece of shit. I just feel like, "Oh, my God. Really?"

Debbie:

It makes you feel bad?

Amanda:

And also, I kinda like the group the way it is. If we start just bringing people in because they're women of color, are

we just bringing in people who don't even really want to do what we want to do? Or who don't ...

Debbie:

And you're worried it might spoil your experience a little bit?

Amanda:

Am I what?

Debbie:

It seems like you're worried that changing the group might affect your own experience a little.

Amanda:

Yes, exactly. I am worried about that. I want it to stay a good place. And I'm open. I'm open to it being better, I'm

open to... I'm not like, "Oh, my gosh, I don't want to have anything new happen in my life."

Debbie:

I'm not sure that I did quite know. I'm certainly hearing that you love this group, and that it's serving you. But something's clearly bothering you about the idea of it changing. And I'm wondering if you can say any more about how it feels when you imagine the group shifting a little?

Amanda:

Okay. So, let's pause there.

Debbie:

Right.

Amanda:

That okay?

Debbie:

Yeah. Please. That's just hard.

Amanda:

Let's pause and hear the three of you guys. What did you observe?

Sam:

Well, it was a little hard to do both the real holding space but also observing and so on. However, it seems like it was helpful for you to have some questions. But it also felt like some of the questions that weren't really about the diversity issue, just took us off on a different track. That you really got on a different path. And then, Debbie said, "Well, but let's come back to this." And then you really opened up more about that, I think. At least it looked like that.

Amanda:

Mm-hmm, mm-hmm, mm-hmm (affirmative). Great. Thank you. What else did you guys see? Doesn't have to be "else." If you saw the same thing, you could say that. But just want to hear what you saw and what it was like for you.

Daniel:

What it was like for me, a little bit, was I was feeling concerned for both people talking in the conversation. I was wanting it to be a good conversation for both of them.

Amanda:

Hmm, hmm, hmm, hmm. And do you think you wanted that because you were holding space for transformation?

Daniel:

Yeah, I think so. Saying the unconditional love, unconditional acceptance. Gets inside and puts the conversation that I'm hearing inside that frame, I guess.

Amanda:

Mm-hmm (affirmative). Mm-hmm (affirmative). Thank you.

Erika:

I saw a real open-hearted-ness. I felt like it got vulnerable pretty quickly. And you willing to admit that you were scared, and her being able to empathize with wanting something from the group experience. "What do you want from the group?" I think, was really drawing out what are your experiences, and caring about those, and not just judging whether what you want is legitimate, but just asking you. And so, it felt like a natural. A little bit back and forth, but her back to you wasn't ping pong. It kept the energy flowing.

So, it felt like you did keep getting deeper, and that you got heard. I think it worked really well.

Amanda:

Mm-hmm, mm-hmm (affirmative). And Debbie, you were the asker. So, did you want to tell us what you noticed, any moments that stood out for you in that exchange, anything you learned in that?

Debbie:

Yes. I noticed, as a whole, that this work is hard for me. I think I have a harder time reading emotions than I do about puzzling out other things. So, this is hard work. When you said that you felt scared, I immediately was worried that *I* had scared you, because I do scare people. And I was thinking maybe I should ask you whether it was my demeanor that was scaring you, or something in the group. It wasn't quite clear. And then I thought of a different way, and I tried to change my body language and say, "Are you feeling scared now?" And I felt like that was a more helpful way of resolving the moment than if I had said, "Did I scare you?" Because then we would've got stuck in something about me, and I actually just found a way out of it. That was quite useful.

But I still don't know whether it was me who scared you, but I do know that we got to a place where you weren't scared, and that's what was important.

Amanda:

And for me, I was surprised that I felt that anxiety ending when you said to me, "Well, what is it that you want to get out of the group, or what is it that you value about the group?" You said something like that. Had me consider more of my own experience. That was a good question because it challenged me to go deeper.

So, I think that was a really good question. And I stopped at a point, Debbie, because there's a little bit of you that resists going into emotions. Is that what you said?

Debbie:

No. I'm pretty comfortable going with emotions. I'm not so good at reading them in other people.

Amanda:

Oh, you're not good at reading them in other people. Okay.

Debbie:

That's right. Mm-hmm (affirmative).

Amanda:

Good. Sometimes I felt like your questions were taking me out of my emotions and into giving you some data. And-

Debbie:

That makes sense.

Amanda:

And this is not a therapy session, but if you can understand where the person is coming from emotionally, then you're probably getting close to what's really at stake for them.

Debbie:

I don't think that I should go in to be a therapist, that would not be my best thing. I'm very good at asking questions to get the data I need. So, that makes sense that I would be doing that. But this is not the time for it, and that's a good lesson.

The Power of Being Transparent about Feelings

Amanda:

The feeling of anxiety hit me so strong, Debbie, I started answering your question. But then I felt like it would be fake if I didn't actually say I felt afraid because it was a big feeling. .

But when you send people into a question about what they really want, or something like that, it can kick up some anxiety, fear, or, "I don't know, what do I really want? Is what I want good?" Right? "Am I going to be judged if I really share what I really want?"

And you said, when you said, "Are you feeling scared now?" You said that, right, Debbie? That was so great. 'Cause I was like, "Okay, no, because you smiled." You let me know, "Okay, we're in this together a little bit."

So, I guess what I'm saying is that if I hadn't told you, "Wow, I feel scared." because I'd come across as confident, you might not have known that. Especially 'cause you're not good at reading emotions.

Debbie:

What I noticed was that it was very helpful for me that you said that you were scared. I don't believe I would've elicited that otherwise. But once I knew, I was able to switch into, "Oh, I know what to do about this. Let me help you not be scared." 'Cause I'm a good mom. But the signal processing is the hard part. So it can be hard to talk to me if I'm not getting the signal. But I'm a good caretaker once I get it.

Step Three: How to Lean In and Move Someone from Head to Heart

Amanda:

Mmm. So, let's do another role play, where we have someone who's more in their head. And I'll play the person who's trying to help you get to the transition from the head to go a little deeper. Or one of you can play that if you feel like you want to give that a try. Whatever you think is going to be most helpful. But this thing about being with people who are in their heads and getting down to their feeling level, it comes up again and again. So, we're going to role play it. I just want to know who wants to do it with me, and which role would you like to play?

Daniel:

I'm typecast being in my head; that one's easy.

Amanda:

Okay, Daniel. This is good. And Daniel, which role do you want to play? Do you want to play the person in the white script in your head, or the racial justice person who's going to be working to help the person move down lower?

Daniel:

The first one.

Amanda:

You're in your head?

Daniel:

Yeah.

Amanda:

Okay, good. So, and for the three of you who are going to watch, if you have an ah-ha, put it in the chat. Okay? So, then, if I feel stuck or something, I can look over to the chat and see suggestions. Even if I don't feel stuck, we can learn from the suggestions as they occur to you in the moment. Okay? Okay. So, Daniel will be someone in his church who's resisting change, and I'll be the Racial Justice Person. You start the role play, Daniel.

Daniel:

Okay. Increasingly, in our Meeting this keeps coming up. We welcome the people of color, but it just seems like we let it keep us from doing our work. We just are all the time fretting over this, and actually we end up acting artificially toward people of color in one way or another. Either we're super effusive, or we're being afraid we're going to say the wrong thing. Or doing things that actually do cause them to feel unwelcome. The more we talk about it, the worse it gets. It doesn't seem like what you guys have come up with so far is going to make it any better.

I'm glad to, I mean, it'd be lovely if this were mostly a congregation of people of color, I'm cool with that. But it doesn't seem like artificially being conscious of it all the time is going to really move things forward. It doesn't seem to have done that so far. We've been putting an amount of effort in it, and it doesn't seem to be getting us anywhere.

Amanda:

Daniel?

Daniel:

Mm-hmm (affirmative).

Amanda:

I just want you to know, I am really listening to you. I really am.

Daniel:

Okay.

Amanda:

When you were looking away, I don't know if you could tell. I want you to know that I am listening to you and I appreciate what you're saying.

Daniel:

Well...I just...it just doesn't seem terribly productive, that's all. It's nothing much more than that. And sometimes even counterproductive.

Amanda:

Sometimes what?

Daniel:

Sometimes even counterproductive.

Amanda:

Oh, counterproductive.

Daniel:

That it actually makes things worse. When we spend so much time on this topic. And there's gotta be a better way. I'm not quite sure what it is. This doesn't seem to be it.

Amanda:

Mmm.

99

Daniel:

I hope some folks can give some thought to that and not just keep doing the same thing you've been doing.

Amanda:

Mm-hmm (affirmative). You said you hope we ...

Daniel:

Give some thought to—

Amanda:

Oh, give some thought.

Daniel:

To listen to this feedback or any other about whether this is making a difference. And like I said, I don't think it is. And then you have some thought if there isn't a better way to be more genuine with people of color that happen to walk in our door, or have been part of our community for a long time. And I'm hoping that...I appreciate the interest in both not hurting the folks that are already here, and not chasing away the folks that come one time. But not this concentrating on it. That doesn't seem to be doing anything very helpful.

Amanda:

Well...I feel sad. How do you feel?

Daniel:

Mm-hmm (affirmative). Well, sadness is—it is frustrating. There's obviously a lot of negativity in the country and we absorb it, but it doesn't look like we can find an answer so yeah, that's sad.

Amanda:

Yeah.

Daniel:

Was there anything else you want to know?

Amanda:

Well...I guess I want to know if you, if we can find a way to work on this together.

Daniel:

It'd just be a guess, I don't know. If there's something that looks like it will actually be productive, it could be, but I genuinely don't know.

Amanda:

Yeah. Well I appreciate your honesty. I mean, I don't know either. But I want us to be a community.

Reflection on the Role Play

Amanda:

Let's take a pause there. Daniel, let's just check in with you. What was that like for you, what did you notice?

Daniel:

Well I noticed at the very end I was tearing up, so I don't know.

Amanda:

You were tearing up?

Daniel:

Yeah. I mean, I was acting I guess generally in a depressed manner, I was becoming more and more clear as I kept talking, that it seemed hopeless to me. And I guess not getting any pushback from my perspective seemed like, "Okay, what's the point?" That I wasn't getting engaged with. I know you said, "I'm listening to you," and I accepted that you were, but it wasn't actual engagement, or it wasn't moving forward, and it was probably making me more depressed at that point.

Amanda:

Yes! Yes, Daniel, yes! How I was being, by not resisting you, you got more depressed. You got more in touch with your own sadness. So rather than me being deflected by you saying "We do this, and they don't come, and da, da, da, and it seems so frustrating." I didn't go for any of those little tidbits that you put out there Daniel, even though in my gut I had some reactions to some of those things, you know?

But I stayed with...I stayed here (hand over heart) and I felt sad. And I felt like I just needed to let you know: I feel sad. And you said, "I feel sad, too." I couldn't tell you were tearing up because your glasses covered it up. But the point in Step Three is not that I somehow make Daniel feel better. I'm not taking care of Daniel, do you see what I mean? I'm not being his shadow, I'm not being his projection. I'm letting him come face to face with something in himself. Which sometimes people resolve by saying, "I don't know what I'm talking about. Whoo! Let me go get some coffee!"

And that might be a successful conversation— "Let me go get some coffee," might be, Wow! Them facing their own discomfort. So let's hear from you guys. Are you okay Daniel?

Daniel:

Yep.

Amanda:

Because I think your sadness was genuine. My sadness was genuine. We're sad at the state of this. So I just want to maybe de-role by maybe taking a moment to honor, and say thank you for being willing to share that.

Amanda:

Okay. Yes. Sam?

Sam:

So I felt like there was this huge shift when you just made that simple naming of sadness. It felt like a seismic shift, not like an earthquake but just like oh, something released, and so it felt like you naming that feeling in yourself, might have opened the door for Daniel to be able to get in touch with what he was feeling, what his emotions were not just this feeling of "nothing's going...we aren't getting anywhere."

Amanda:

Thank you, Sam. And I want to say something about that, "We're not getting anywhere." Because I'm someone who's maybe triggered by that statement. People say, "We're not getting anywhere," I get mad. And if I had gotten mad and said, "Well Daniel, we've made all these changes...," what do you think Daniel would have done? Anybody want to guess, if I had come up with that?

Sam:

Argued.

Amanda:

Yeah, he would have said "Yeah, but..."

Sam:

"Yeah, but nothing has really changed."

Amanda:

Right! And then we're off to the races. And I'm still sad and he's still sad, but we're *arguing*. Mave we it's easier to argue than to really feel the sad, scary, hopeless feeling.

What else?

Debbie:

So it was a really powerful shift, I noticed that. And just observing Daniel, it was really hard to remember that he was role playing. It was clear that he was living this, even if on the other side of it—it feels like it was real. And I felt personally sort of relieved—it was like we brought Daniel into feeling. That was the idea, "Let's get out of our heads and into what's real." And there was this moment, Daniel, I don't know whether I saw that you were tearing up—it's almost like I don't read emotions until I do, and then I'm like, "oh! I'm with you!" So I wrote that I wanted to say, "I'm feeling for you right now, and I'm sorry this feels so hard." Like, "Oh my gosh, you're doing the work and I'm here for you right now.

Daniel:

Cool.

Amanda:

Consider this in the spirit of experimentation: What is it like for you to just *be* those words when you're talking to someone without saying them? Daniel, if you had heard me say, "I'm feeling for you right now, or I'm sorry this feels so hard?" how might that have impacted you?

Daniel:

I think saying that you were sad and that I seemed sad was probably more effective than saying that you were feeling for me. The descriptive thing worked better than saying that.

Amanda:

Daniel, what if I had said, after I had established that I feel sad, and you said you felt sad, what if I had then said something like, "I'm feeling for you," or, "I'm sorry this feels hard"?

Daniel:

I guess I would have said something like, "Yeah, it's frustrating. We don't seem to know what to do." I mean I would have responded to it, but I'm not wanting you to feel sorry for me, I guess. So I don't think it would be particularly well received. It wouldn't be off putting particularly, but it wouldn't move anything with me.

Amanda:

Okay, thank you.

Daniel:

Yeah.

Amanda:

Thank you for checking in on that. Now let's look at the real time suggestions that you all wrote in the chat. I'm laughing, Erika because I'm looking at your suggested question: "What do you imagine it could be like to be able to be 'more genuine' with people of color?"

Erika:

It's so heady!

Amanda:

That's exactly it. You took the bait, Erika.

Erika:

I did. I see it now.

Amanda:

Yes you went for his words, rather than for what was feeling underneath there, and Erika I know you, I know how quickly you can feel people.

Erika:

I was hearing him yearn to be more genuine, and I was kind of wanting to explore that. What is it that this might feel like? So sort of that idea of a vision of blessed community, I guess that's where I was, but when I read that question now I can see that I was just going to go into that head thing.

The other thing I definitely felt was this sense of hopelessness, and I love the way that you answered, but I wondered, if you didn't have that insight, and what you picked up on was the hopelessness, what would you do with that? In some ways it feels like a dead end. Like, "Wow. It sounds like you feel really hopeless about this," and then what?

Amanda:

Okay so two things. One is, it is not bad for people to feel hopeless because the situation is not a great situation, right? And if you want to activate people, sometimes they have to feel the pain of where they're at. Also, it's not your responsibility to resolve their pain in a conversation.

And number two, you don't have to do it all in one conversation. That thing that you wanted to get to, Erika— "sounds like you're yearning for…", "what would it look like…", I wouldn't go there in this conversation. But you can have another one. For someone who spends a lot of time in their head, just getting to the heart, and having them be with that discomfort, is *huge*. Because they got to a feeling level. And you could check in with them again, in however much time you feel is right.

"How are you today? How are you feeling?" You could actually say, "How are you feeling since that conversation we had?"

So all right. Cool.

Step Three is the hardest step, honestly. So I'm good with us spending this time on it because the nuances are coming out in this call that we haven't really been able to pull out before.

Sam, I'm wondering what's rising up for you? You haven't said anything in a while. I'm just wondering what's opening up for you, what questions you're having.

Sam:

I'm uncharacteristically quiet (laughs). No, I was just taking all that in and finding it really helpful. And actually I found Erika's naming of yearning really resonated for me, because I feel that often—just a yearning for connection. Somebody told me a quote something like, "What everybody really wants in life is to be met, and to be seen."

Anyway, so that's what part of what was coming up for me.

And then the other thing is about saying sympathetic words like, "I'm sorry this feels so hard," and, "I'm feeling for you right now." Something I have learned is that when you're trying to connect with somebody and you say I'm sorry, there's sort of a power differential. I feel sorry *for* you. That's sympathy, but what we really want is empathy, feeling together. So that's why "I'm feeling sad," and then him saying, "I feel sad, too,"—that was empathy. That was really connecting those emotions, without Daniel feeling like, "Well, I don't want you to feel *sorry* for me." So those were the things that came up for me.

Amanda:

Thank you. Right, thank you so much. I want to expand on this thing (repeats Sam's gesture of hands on two different levels). In Step Three, when you first start doing it, you can find yourself assuming a little bit of this upper hand thing, like being a little condescending or therapeutic. So if you can be with your own feelings, notice them, and share them, and check in how the other person is feeling, it's a way to not do it like that (gesturing with hands on two different levels).

And to model being vulnerable and taking risks.

And the other thing that you said Sam, the reason why I clapped, is because you just transitioned us to Step Four where I could have said to Daniel, "Would you like to hear what it's like for me?" And Daniel, in that state he was in, he might have really said, "Yes."

And then it would have made sense—for me to share my yearning, like where you were starting to go, Erika, in expressing what you're yearning for. The lessons I want us to take from this role play is, don't go for the bait. Don't go for the stuff, you know, when your kids or your spouse they put that stuff outside the door to distract you. They're not doing it on purpose, but you know, yeah—*go deeper*. And the more in touch you are with your feelings, the more present you can be with the other person.

And for those people who tell me, "Amanda I'm too emotional. I can't have these conversations, because I'm too emotional." I say, your emotions are a great gift. If you're not fighting them, if they're not completely in charge, if you've done some work with them, or if you continuously tend to your emotions, they're a great strength.

Let's take a pause here to drink some water and digest what we're learning.

ACTION STEP:

Take a few minutes to review the **"Lean In Checklist"** below.

STEP THREE: A Lean-In Checklist

- **Lean In with questions.** Why do you feel that way? Can you say more about that?

- **Lean In with feelings.** Keep breathing into your heart. Repeat the feeling words that someone shares. Say out loud what you're feeling.

- **Lean In with discomfort**. When we leave someone with tension or when we help someone to experience their discomfort, that can inspire them to actively seek out solutions.

STEP FOUR: PLANT A SEED

Amanda:

So let's go to Step Four.

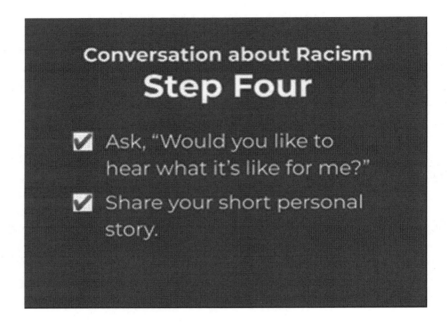

So Step Four is where you get to Plant a Seed. You ask, "Would you like to hear what it's like for me?" If the

person says yes, then you share a seed, something brief, heartfelt, and then you drop the mic.

Why Ask if They Want to Hear from You?

I ask"Would you like to hear what it's like for me?" so that I don't speak to people who don't want to hear from

me. Very simply, please don't waste your time and precious energy on someone who does not want to hear from you. Think about my earlier role play with Daniel. Had he said, "No, I don't want to hear from you," who would have benefitted from me sharing my heart with him? We get into escalated conflicts when we chase somebody and demand that they listen. "Hey, you better listen to me!"

Reflect on your own experience. Did someone really listen when you coerced or presumed upon them? Think about your child or spouse. Even people who already love you can't be forced to listen to you with an open mind and heart. When presumed or forced, the best case scenario is that they'll fake listen, or the worst is that they absolutely resist by walking away or speaking on top of you. Therefore, when you are in a difficult conversation about racism, we want to make sure that the person is willing to give us their attention before we speak. We want their investment in listening.

And what I have found is that if you're pursuing somebody, you're definitely in the weaker position. If you're being pursued, meaning they *want* to hear from you, then they're going to value whatever you have to say. So the best position to be in in a conversation is when someone says, "Would you tell me, share what it's like for you? Will you tell me what you think? Please share with me where you're coming from." Because then they want to know. The trick is not to tell them everything you know; instead put down just enough to plant a seed.

Why Be Brief?

And then the reason why I say share something brief and heartfelt and drop the mic, is that in my experience I can't explain 400 years of American history in one setting. I can't explain mass incarceration and summarize Michelle Alexander's book, *The New Jim Crow,* in one setting. I'm not even an expert in mass incarceration. You know what I mean? I'm not an expert in affirmative action. I'm not an expert in so many subjects. I don't really know that much about the NFL. And I haven't done studies on athletes who take a stand during games, or take a knee. There are lots of books on all these things, and I haven't read most of them. In a conversation where I'm leaning in and planting a seed, I don't need a whole slew of facts to impact somebody. When they've done studies about what makes people change their minds, they found that the most powerful factors are repetition and emotional connection. It's repetition and stuff that gets to their hearts. So you can let go of the belief that if you just had more facts, you would have changed somebody's mind.

When you put down just enough to plant a seed, then you give the other person some space to take responsibility to learn more. When you try to give them the whole history of mass incarceration, then you're not helping them. You know you're not encouraging them to take responsibility. Instead, you might be trying to force feed them. The Lean In and Plant a Seed approach is not about you dominating or beating somebody in a verbal duel to determine who is smarter or more right or better. Rather, we are looking to connect and drop a seed that can eventually disrupt their whole outlook.

Another reason to plant a seed is that sharing more often translates into people of color overfunctioning in these conversations or in relationships with European American folks. It's very easy to do. It can be very seductive when someone says, "Amanda, tell me this." And you want to, you know? But really, people can read on their own. They can go check out the film, the article, or the audiobook. Let them do some work. They will retain more when they actively acquire information. Most importantly, it's harmful for people of color to rehearse their racial trauma solely for a European American's education. All too often, Black and Latino professionals in predominantly white spaces tell me they are exhausted and resentful of "bleeding" so that their colleagues can learn. In my Tedx Talk, "How to Lean In to Conversations about Racism" I describe a conversation where I planted a seed rather than catalogue all of my hurts to a skeptical European American colleague. As God-Is would have it, that colleague resurfaced while editing this book, and told me that that conversation changed his life.

So I tell people, "Don't worry about trying to give them everything. Give them a little something." Then you can always follow up with the link for other things that they could do. You could send them to dramandakemp.com for free classes and resources. You could give them announcements about meetings or speakers. Do you get the flavor of what I'm saying? Okay, good. So let's turn to identifying a story that could be your seed.

ACTION STEP:

Develop your own seed-planting story by completing "**Worksheet for Step Four: Plant a Seed**" below.

Worksheet for Step Four: Plant a Seed

1. Write about a time when you realized you had internalized a negative racial stereotype.

_____

_____

_____

_____

_____

2. How has racism personally harmed you or a loved one?

_____

_____

_____

_____

_____

3. What's one situation where you regret how you handled a racial dynamic?

_____

_____

_____

_____

4. What would it be like if you could share any of these incidents with a racial justice community or mentor?

_____

_____

_____

_____

Finding your seed-planting story

Amanda:

So you were asked to consider something from your own story that explains why you're so committed to racial justice. Something personal and heartfelt. So I'd like to hear from one person and give some feedback. Then I'll put you in pairs, and then you can give each other feedback. So we need somebody willing to share so the whole group can learn. Yay! Thanks, Sam!

Sam:

Okay. So after Michael Brown was killed and Eric Garner was killed and Trayvon Martin had been killed a couple of years prior, I was connecting with classmates from college on Facebook. These were people that I feel are exactly like me. They grew up middle class, upper middle class. They went to the same highly competitive, elite liberal arts college I went to. They are doctors. They are lawyers. And they are also Black. And then I realized when I found out from them that when they have "the Conversation" with their teenage sons and daughters, it was not about—as mine was—about safe sex, consent, drugs and alcohol. Those sort of things. They had to tell their children how to behave when they get stopped by the police so they don't get killed. So they don't get shot. I lost it. It was, it was like a kick in the stomach or a kick in the head.

Amanda:

Hmm. Hmm. So, so now I'm going to give some feedback. I want to say that at the very end I had an emotional reaction when you said, "I lost it." I kind of leaned in to find out more. And you described it as like "a kick in the head, a kick in the stomach." My next instinct was I want to hear more about that. I would have asked you more about that, or I would've wondered even if I didn't ask. But the piece about the selective, highly selective liberal arts colleges and that kind of thing was a little distracting and *off putting*. But "I lost it." I think a statement about your loss—like how it personally woke you up or made you look at everything—I think that would be helpful.

So let's just take a breath. "What questions are coming up for you?" Questions or comments. Yeah, Debbie?

Debbie:

I guess the question that comes up for me was, "What did you think before?"

Amanda:

So, that might be another way to frame it: "Before the killing of Trayvon and Mike Brown, (and the litany that you went on), I thought X, and then after that I thought Y."

ACTION STEP:

Journal about one thing you are taking away from this teaching on Seed Planting.

STEP FIVE: REFLECT ON YOURSELF

Conversation about Racism
Step Five

☑ Reflect on yourself.
☑ Where do you need help?

Amanda:

Now we're going to focus on Step Five in the process to Lean In and Plant a Seed. Remember, Step One is to Check in with your Wise Self. Step two is to Hold Space for Transformation. Step Three is where you Lean In and really *listen*...but listen in a wholly new way than we normally do; to really get the perspective of that person, and to ask questions that help to get them from their heads to their hearts, to help you see, and help them articulate their values. And then Step Four is to Plant a Seed by asking, "Would you like to hear what it is like for me?" And once that person tells you, "Yes," then you share that short, powerful story that captures what it's like for you when you are dealing with racism, white supremacy, and/or whiteness. But then you're not done, because Step Five is to Reflect on Yourself.

Reflecting is critical because this is where you get to integrate some learning. The first thing I want you to do when you reflect on yourself is to acknowledge yourself. You showed up. You extended yourself. You opened up. You practiced something that is counter-cultural. So find something to acknowledge yourself for *no matter what*—no matter how imperfectly you did these steps or whatever the outcome was.

Why Acknowledge Yourself?

Acknowledgment is more than making yourself feel good. Although making yourself feel good *is* part of your birthright. You know, we're on this planet, I think, to grow and to stretch, but we're also here to enjoy, to experience pleasure. I think Adrienne Maree Brown's new book2 is something about—you know, *joy* and pleasure in the course of being an agent for social change. So making yourself feel good is legit. Acknowledging yourself is also part of creating an alternative culture—within your system, but also within your other groupings. A culture of appreciation flies in the face of perfectionism. Capitalism and white supremacy *generate* a kind of anxiety to *acquire*, to always do better, and better, and better. Well, acknowledging actually just breaks you out of that automatic, inclination. (Inhales.) Mm. And just accepting yourself. And just as I asked you to plant a seed in Step Four, when you acknowledge yourself, you're watering your own seed, the seed of the beautiful being that you're evolving into in Step Five..

So that's the first part of your reflection. The second part of your reflection would be to actually consider: What were the emotions and the physical sensations that you experienced as you had that conversation? So I've had people tell me literally things like, "Well, I felt off balance." "I notice myself pulling back." "I flew out of my body," or, "I noticed that my breath got slower." All of those kinds of things are important cues for you. What we know about human beings and transformation work is that it's *embodied*. And when we slip out of our bodies or when we don't notice what our bodies are reacting to or how our bodies are responding in a given situation, we're missing out on vital information—maybe about the other person—but a lot of times about ourselves. So for example, I noticed—I was facilitating a group yesterday—and I noticed that, looking back on it, that my breath was in my chest a lot yesterday. And I didn't often slow down for the belly breath.

And what that tells me is that in this particular situation, I was *afraid* to really sink in with this group. I was afraid that they would find me too...crunchy, woo-woo, spiritual. And because of my fear of their judgment, I had this tightness inside me. And so my breath was up here. Now with that information, with the help of someone else, I can talk it through about why I felt the group would find me too, whatever-it-is. I could also make a commitment to myself, to be unique and wonderful in a group, even if that wasn't their dominant culture, you know? I could make a commitment to myself that I'm not going to leave myself just because I'm afraid other people won't join me.

Share with a Skilled Mentor or Friend

So I mentioned sharing with another person because this is another part of a reflecting on yourself. Absolutely we need to do reflection on our own, *and* it's really helpful, especially for those of us who are extroverts, to have another person to process with, to externalize the reflection process. Because for extroverts we often don't know what we've learned until we try to communicate it to someone else.

So who could you reflect on yourself with that will do more than let you vent? I want you to choose someone who has an idea of what it means to Hold Space for Transformation and Lean in and listen to you. Wouldn't it be great if you could say to a trusted mentor or friend, "I'd like to talk for like maybe five minutes without interruption. I'm just going to set my timer and just say, 'Here's what I noticed about myself.'"

Choose someone who you can *ask* for what you want. And *be clear* about what it is you're asking for. In Racial Justice from the Heart programs, we train our mentors and participants to Hold Space for transformation and Lean In so that you can encounter your truth, and your lessons. Just as we discovered in the chapter on Leaning In, timely organic questions can help you to see more, that you may not initially see when you first look back at a situation.

I'm going to give you an example. I was having a call with Ginger, and she shared about a specific incident where she didn't use their voice, where she felt silenced. And so what we did was in the reflecting yourself part is we went back and looked at what was happening in their body when she went silent, when she felt shut down. And then we did a role play where the incident occurred but she accessed parts of her body that felt strong, that give her a sense of strength and groundedness.

So in my case, my hands feel magical to me. And, so one of my tools when I feel scared is to come back to my hands. To *trust* my hands, you know. To really be conscious of what my hands are doing. And you see my hands are very active in this video with you.

Give Yourself What You Need

And then finally, when you reflect, ask yourself, "What do I need now?" Do I need to forgive myself for where I slipped up, or where I didn't go as far as I could have gone? Do I need to forgive myself for saying yes to the conversation? Do I need to do some journaling about whatever triggered me in an interaction? Do I need to explore what part of me believes or shares a value that I detest? What do I need to extend kindness to myself? Whatever it is, ask yourself what you need, and then give it to yourself. Sometimes what we need is a bath. We need, you know, we need to put our feet in some salt water, even if we don't have time for a whole bath. Mmm. Sometimes we need a glass of water, of really pure, energized water.

I mentioned forgiveness because so often that is what we need. And I use the Ho'oponopono meditation/prayer. I have a version of it on my *Black Girl Magic* album, but the Ho'oponopono phrases are, "I'm sorry. Please forgive me. Thank you. I love you." And I like to do it while caressing my arm. "I'm sorry. Please forgive me. Thank you. I love you. I'm sorry. Please forgive me, Amanda. Thank you. I love you." And that very gentle prayer helps me to be with whatever feelings have arisen from, you know, the conversation. It helps me to be present to myself and to know that I'm willing to be gentle and kind to myself as I evolve. And that is the truth about this whole thing. We're all evolving. None of us is the expert, the final product, in this area or maybe any other area. We're all evolving. And so since we're all evolving and we're never going to be 100% perfect, why don't we love ourselves along the way? Why don't we give ourselves some comfort and some pleasure, as we do that evolutionary work?

On that note, we are coming to a close. *Thank you* for reading this book. Thank you for being committed to having this new kind of conversation about racism. Thank you for being open to transformation.

If you would like to have some one-on-one time to talk about a place where you're stuck, or where you would like to really make a difference, please contact us. We have a Racial Justice Breakthrough sessions, especially for people who are deeply called to racial justice work. If you have a spiritual calling to work for justice and compassion, we want to support you.

ACTION STEP:

Complete **"Worksheet for Step Five: Reflect on Yourself"** below.

Worksheet for Step Five: Reflect on Yourself

1. Why is acknowledging yourself important? Would you like to make a habit of appreciating yourself? Why or why not?

_____

_____

_____

2. Recall a recent conversation about racism or something similar. What body sensations do you remember? How was your breathing?

_____

_____

_____

_____

3. What can you learn from your emotions or your body sensations about your own areas for continued growth?

_____

_____

_____

_____

4. Ask yourself what you need after that conversation. Write it down, no matter how small or big.

_____

_____

_____

_____

5. Do you have a trusted mentor or buddy who can help you reflect on yourself? If you were to apply for a free racial justice breakthrough session, what would you want help with?

_____

_____

_____

_____

Reflect on your Self-Care Experience

ACTION STEP:

Do one self care practice. Try the Body Scan from the *Black Girl Magic* album.

Amanda:

Okay, so, welcome back everybody. Hope you had a good break. So, to start with, let's just check in on what self-care/meditative practice you did during the break. Who'd be willing to share? Just raise your hand. Okay, great. Daniel, let us know what you did. You have to unmute yourself.

Daniel:

Actually, I saw down at the end that you had Ho'oponopono, which I'm familiar with from past trainings and using it. So, that's what I focused on—going through that exercise and seeing how it varied from what I get out on the Insight Timer meditation app. So that's about it.

Amanda:

So how are feeling now? Having done the Ho'oponopono?

Daniel:

It was good, and it was helpful. I also returned a phone call, which I probably shouldn't have (laughs). But it was helpful to see it in the light of what you were saying about the "*Black Girl Magic* and me" kinda thing. It helped me figure out how to deal with the fact that I don't identify in either of those categories and how to make use of it, so I appreciate that.

Amanda:

Mm-hmm (affirmative) Awesome, thank you Daniel. And I appreciate that you had to make a phone call. So, with these brief meditation practices, sometimes you've got 15 minutes and then you have to make a phone call, you know, or go back to whatever it is that you need to put your attention to. So, thank you.

Debbie, you want to unmute yourself and let us know what you did?

Debbie:

Yeah, I did Ho'oponopono too. I've heard it one time before because I've been listening to your recording, so I recognized it and thought I would use that, which was nice. I needed to close my eyes for a few minutes 'cause I got up very early, so I did that. And make my feet warm. I work from home, and I have a colleague just arrived, so I checked in with her. Was just checking how her training was going. So, now she's a presence in my house but my door was closed, so that was kinda nice to set her up.

Amanda:

Nice. And you got your feet warm?

Debbie:

Yeah, my feet get cold. And I got plenty of water.

Amanda:

Awesome. Great. Sam?

Sam:

Well, the third time's the charm; I did Ho'oponopono also. And actually, it was in my mind and heart that I wanted to do that practice. First, I had to attend to a few other things of self-care and, you know, bodily functions and things like that. And then after I answered an urgent email that was originally a phone call that I ignored, I said, "Okay, I really need this practice." And so I said, "I'll listen to it on *Black Girl Magic*," and so that was really lovely. It was really good. There must be something magical that we all three did that!

Amanda:

Yes. Yes. I think, especially 'cause I didn't point you towards it at all, so I'm interested in how that's going to, you know, infuse the rest of our time together. Erika, how about you? What did you do?

Erika:

I did the body scan on *Black Girl Magic*…I loved the way you introduced that as sort of giving you an alternative focus from where your brain goes and being in your head. Of course, my head is still multitasking part of the time, but…I was amazed, you know, you finish that and it's only 11, 12 minutes, and wow there's still time. You know, when I'm surfing the internet, it's amazing how that time just kind of slips and gets frittered away into, you know, I don't even know where it went but it doesn't feel that dense with helpful nourishment. So, that was really nice.

Amanda:

Yes, yes …Awesome, awesome. So, today, we're going to have several breaks and I wanted you to be aware of those breaks in there. Because if you think about what Step One is in the system, Step One is to check in with your wise self to see if you're balanced. And if you have a regular practice of self-care, you know, some kind of meditation that helps you restore you to balance to get you back into your body, or to let go and to process hurts, then you're more likely to be ready, you know, when the time comes.

Self-care Check In

Amanda:

Okay. So I want to do a self-care check in, because I told you I was going to check on you after the lunch break. Daniel laughed, but I was serious. Sometimes it's accountability that actually makes us do the thing that is ultimately very good for us. So I just want to check in: what self care things have you done over the last two breaks? So who would like to start?

And this is going to be just a brief check in. I'll call on you. Sam what did you do? If anything?

Sam:

I went for a walk.

Amanda:

Aw, good for you. Awesome. Thank you. So the thing about walking, obviously, is moving the body, getting back into the body, but one of the big things they say for like composting stress, is being in nature. Is like actually, physically giving over. If you can put your feet on the actual ground—barefoot being the best way to do that.

Sam:

I did not go barefoot, but for those who don't know where I live, the Appalachian Trail is about a 100 yards away, up the hill through the forest from my complex where I live. The trees are right there breathing at me all the time.

Amanda:

Awesome. Good, good, good. Okay great. Debbie, what did you do?

Debbie:

I made tea, which is always good for me. I didn't feel like I had time for a nap. I, actually in the middle of the last session, got a text with like, "Call me because I have some bad news I have to tell you," so I followed up on that. And the good news is it was not as bad as I thought, but I had to spend 10 minutes kind of absorbing some bad news that someone had to tell me, and that was it. I was in a really good place to do it. My son came home from school and I took care of him, took care of some things he needs, checked in with him. So it was a moment of self care, and also quite a bit of being a community member and a mom, all packed in. Oh, and I had a banana.

Amanda:

Awesome, thank you. Erika what did you do?

Erika:

At the first break I went for a walk with my dogs around the block, even though it was raining, but that was nice. And made myself some coffee. And the second break I sat with my kitty and was just chilling with him. And I knitted for a little bit.

Amanda:

Okay, I just want to say that's another thing that they found actually de-stresses people, is touching your pets.

Erika:

Amen.

Amanda:

Great. How about you Daniel?

Daniel:

I talked to my wife, and we shared what we'd each been doing for the past several hours. And then I also explored your *Black Girl Magic* tracks. Especially the Feel Flow one. First couple of times, I was analytic, and then I tried to let it, just be with it for some time. This last time, the Friends Journal had come in the mail, which was all about Quaker humor this time, if there is such a thing. And lots of snacking, too.

Amanda:

Awesome. Great. And I did a body scan. It was good. I'm tired. This is *work!* Okay, good.

AFTERWORD

I hope the tools in this workbook have helped you to have difficult conversations. I know it's not easy to take on something that terrifies you. Please remember that it's okay to take it a little bit at a time. In fact, as a mentor I want you to know that I encourage my clients to NOT undertake a conversation if it puts them in a panic zone. Rather, I suggest you take a step that stretches you without overwhelming your body with the chemicals that come from fear.

In that vein I encourage you to get a mentor for your racial justice work. A mentor can save you a lot of suffering and paralysis and help you to take actions that are right for YOU--not some other person. I'm going to focus the rest of this afterword on the benefits of mentorship because I know that a mentor can help you put the theory in this book into practice and get deeper and faster results.

So, what is a mentor?

First, a mentor is not a coach. You know how in athletics there's a coach, and there's an athlete? The athlete is on the court or on the ice and the coach is on the side, right? Well, not a mentor. Mentoring means I'm on the court too. I'm also at risk. I am failing as well as succeeding. And as a mentor, I investigate my failures and share them with you. So I'm promising to be constantly learning. And, maybe I'm a little bit ahead of you. I think everybody should have somebody who's a little bit ahead of them. But I am human, and I don't pretend to be perfect at that, which I am practicing.

Second, you get the most benefit from mentors who are actively and specifically guiding you. In my case this involves a monetary exchange because I do it as a profession. When someone knows your story and the goals or negative core beliefs you are carrying, they can catch you before you spiral into a pattern. I've invested thousands of dollars and hours in mentors because I needed clarity and emotional support to walk the path of racial justice and mindfulness as a business and as a way of being in the world. Whether I exchanged money, time or just heartfelt thanks, the more each of us invested in the relationship, the more I got out of it.

Third, you can also have mentors who don't even know that they're mentoring you because you read their books; you listen to all their stuff online; or you go to all their courses. If you liked this book, I encourage you to get in Racial Justice from the Heart world. Read my other books and blog, or subscribe to Dr. Amanda Kemp YouTube channel, and check out all those videos. I'm happy to mentor you through all the freebie routes.

However, if you decide you want to make a commitment to honestly and deliberately investigate your hidden biases or wherever it is that you're stuck, then reach out to us. We've created the Stop Being Afraid in 5 Steps online course as a next step from this workbook, and it includes group coaching and practice calls. We also provide private mentorship to a small group of highly motivated people of European descent and to Black and Indigenous leaders of color. Just go to: dramandakemp.com/contact.

ALSO BY DR. AMANDA KEMP

You can find these at amandakemp.bandcamp.com

Say the Wrong Thing: Stories and Strategies for Racial Justice and Authentic Community

Black Girl Magic: Poems, Meditations and Spells

Show me the Franklins! A play about the Ancestors, Slavery and Benjamin Franklin

Inspira: The Power of the Spiritual

Chaconne Emancipated, Violin and Spoken Word Collaboration with Michael Jamanis

ACKNOWLEDGEMENTS

This publication would not have been possible without the careful editing and affirmation of Dr. Erika Fitz, Senior Trainer in Racial Justice from the H.e.a.r.t.. She tirelessly and diligently applied herself to this project and for this I am grateful.

I also want to affirm Natalie Sanchez, a theatre artist and social justice writer who has served as a virtual assistant for Racial Justice from the Heart since our early days. Natalie's commitment and groundedness was clutch.

I truly appreciate all of the people of faith, students, and educators who have trusted me to mentor them and been willing to share their lives with me.

Finally, I acknowledge my ancestors, biological and spiritual, who have watched over me and helped to mend my heart.

Made in the USA
Las Vegas, NV
28 August 2021